NOT PAID

ELEVEN CENTS

AN HOUR

TO THINK

For Mike H.

MY EXPERIENCES OF

THE VIETNAM WAR

AND OTHER STORIES

Jim Gibson

Jim Gibson

ACORN
PUBLISHING

www.acornpublishingllc.com
For information, address:
Acorn Publishing, LLC
3943 Irvine Blvd. Ste. 218
Irvine, CA 92602
Not Paid Eleven Cents an Hour To Think:My Experiences of the
Vietnam War and Other Stories

Hardcover: 978-1-952112-92-8
Paperback: 978-1-952112-91-1

TABLE OF CONTENTS

For Gale, Annie, and John

Dust Off at Bearcat

Evacuating the wounded, Vietnam 1969

INTRODUCTION

LIFE TAKES US into the unknown where we begin our journeys with small steps into the mystery of what lies ahead, unaware of the things influencing our past. We come into this world, not knowing from one moment to the next what is going to happen to us. Did we ask for this? I don't think so, and I don't believe in God or preordination. Things just happen, and we try to make the best of whatever life presents us with. I think this is the basic truth of existence—we just try to make the best of things as they come.

I have written this book for you to be able to understand what can happen. If we are not careful, the wrong people and forces can take control and wreak horrible consequences. This book is especially intended for young minds who might want to know about these things.

My mother kept the letters I sent her and my father when I was in Vietnam. I base much of the chronology in the second part of this book on the memories rekindled by those letters. This story is about something that happened to me as a young man and how I tried to make the best of it. It's the story of my Vietnam War experiences, told in three parts. In part one, I describe my childhood and many experiences growing up until my life was interrupted by the War. Part two is comprised of the stories of my experiences of the War while on the ground with the Army in Vietnam. Part three is about my life as a Vietnam

Veteran, my return to Vietnam, and my recovery from the War. I have changed the names of many individuals and described several circumstances throughout this book in ways to provide respect and privacy for those involved. Otherwise, it exists as it is, exactly from memory.

I must advise the reader that some of the scenes and events in this book contain graphic violence and examples of horrific human behavior that might be upsetting to those of us who have lived our lives in a normal civilized world; many of my experiences of the Vietnam War were not those experienced in a normal civilized world. Also, I describe a few conversations that may seem disturbing and inappropriate. This is because my intention is to describe these conversations verbatim, as I actually heard them.

Art and painting have always occupied a central place in my life. I have included in my narrative several depictive original oil paintings from my "Vietnam War Series."

PRELUDE

December 1, 1968

I WAS ON this huge airliner flying into what I thought could be the end of my life.

By "huge airliner," I mean a Stretch DC8, one of the biggest flight vehicles in the world. I was among about 225 other young soldiers flying west over the Pacific Ocean, headed for Vietnam on this military-chartered jet aircraft. Our country was losing sometimes five hundred soldiers a week at that point. I was twenty years old, an Army Private E-1, a trained Combat Medic, dressed in brand new, scratchy, combat jungle fatigues, wearing a pair of brand new, uncomfortable combat jungle boots. Most of us kids were scared to death. Some were sniffling and crying as we started our descent into Vietnam. I wasn't afraid as I sat there in my seat and read *The Aquarian Gospel of Jesus the Christ*.

After a while, the sound system came on and the pilot told us we were soon to land. He told us to prepare ourselves as the aircraft would have to make a steep, radical dive as it approached the runway and that he would then have to, in a similar manner, bring the plane's nose up just before landing. This to avoid being hit by enemy fire. The officer of the flight then came on and told us we were to get off the plane rapidly once we landed, then quickly make our way to a nearby concrete bunker. We were told to wait there for further instructions.

The officer had given us his orderly instructions but as soon as the plane landed and the doors opened, other voices commanded us: "Get out! Get out! *Get out!* Move! Move! *Move!* Get your asses off this plane! Now!"

There was a lot of pushing and shoving. The line of soldiers shuffled forward, and I moved with the rest until I was there at the doorway where we were practically being thrown off the plane. As I began moving out of the air-conditioned plane and down the ramp, I was hit with what seemed to me a blast furnace of humid air. Once on the ground, I was also greeted with an awful, nauseating smell. Somebody said it was the scent of burning shit. Oil barrels, cut in half, filled with soldiers' shit soaked in diesel fuel and lit on fire.

The jet's engines roared as the pilot began moving the plane down the runway to make room for the next transport coming right up behind him. I followed others to a bunker, then sat on my duffle bag in the heat. Men were running around yelling. Loud booming noises came from different directions off in the distance. It was getting dark.

There was a continuous loud sound of something like *whomp* you could feel coming from all directions. You could feel it in your bones. Helicopter blades thudded in the distance. It was then that an intense fear consumed me as I realized the absolutely insane madness that I had descended into.

This was Vietnam.

PART ONE:

THE AMERICAN DREAM

CHAPTER 1

The American Dream

I WAS SEVEN years old in the summer of 1955 when my father's company assigned him to a new sales territory in Orange County, California. He worked for a Los Angeles food brokerage firm selling food products to markets throughout Southern California. My family then moved south, from the beautiful coastal City of Santa Barbara, where I had been born in 1948, to what was then one of the orange-growing capitals of America.

Anaheim was a rapidly expanding city where we settled into a new housing project just before Disneyland opened its doors to the public later that summer. Our nearly new, three-bedroom, two-bath tract home was typical of the hundreds of thousands of tract homes built in the cities and towns of Southern California to accommodate the masses of workers flowing into the state with its booming economy.

Housing developments were going up overnight in Orange County as the citrus growers sold off their groves, making fortunes. Bulldozers would uproot the orange trees and pile them in enormous stacks which were then doused with gasoline and set on fire. Anaheim had a population of twenty-five thousand in 1955, and by 1960 it would grow to over one hundred thousand. Our tract, like so many, was hewn from the groves.

There was a tall cinder block wall on our housing tract's west side with Gilbert Street running alongside it. This wall and street separated and shielded our brand-new tract development, where only white people lived, from a Mexican barrio where only brown people lived. The block wall barrier had only one street opening that provided access to both communities. The orange grove owners had established the barrio known as *"La Colonia de Independencia"* in 1914, a citrus camp for Mexican workers who hand-picked the oranges for wealthy white families. In time, it had grown into a little town of its own.

The white growers, through their benevolence, had also established Magnolia School #2, within the barrio, shortly after the camp came into existence, as a schoolhouse for Mexican kids only. Segregation was strictly adhered to, so Mexican kids went to their brown schools while white kids were sent to white schools. By the time my family moved into our tract home in 1955, California had begun to desegregate its schools. White kids and Mexican kids were then required to attend the same schools, meaning Magnolia School #2 in the barrio is where I started the second grade. I recall walking out of our tract with my brother Billy through the lone street opening to get to the school. This different neighborhood interested my seven-year-old self; it had dirt roads, no sidewalks, fences, or lawns, but colorful flowering cactuses grew between its houses; dogs, cats, and chickens roamed freely. The old schoolhouse had a bell tower and its classrooms had cloakrooms; the desks sat on wrought iron rails, the old-fashioned kind, with inkwells. Every day, we happily walked back and forth between our neighborhoods to school, and we never gave a thought to any differences between our Mexican friends and our white friends. We played together and had fun, as kids do, and that was that.

A year later, my family moved again, this time to a housing tract on the other side of Anaheim to Alden Avenue. Just three houses down from our house, the orange groves, ranches, and farms began and stretched to the east uninterrupted for miles and miles. As a kid, my days were spent running through the orange groves, playing with my brother Billy and our friends. We would roam in packs, throwing fresh oranges at each other from forts we made. We would also sneak in and explore the many tract home construction sites after the workers would go home for the night. It was paradise growing up there.

I was the youngest of four children from a stable working-to-middle class white family, living in a white suburban neighborhood in Orange County. Dad's company always made sure that their sales reps drove brand-new cars. My mom was an elementary school teacher who loved her job. Life was good and we had little to complain about. We were all living the American Dream.

There was no reason for me to question anything. I was just an average kid entering junior high in the seventh grade, growing up in sunny suburban Southern California, where people were people, and things were what they were. My main interests in life were football and art. I loved playing football and drawing cartoons. We invented skateboards and lived our lives as sidewalk surfers. I didn't think of myself as a white kid, and I didn't think of my Mexican friends as Mexicans either. That is, until one day I noticed some of my school buddies seemed to be looking down on some of my Mexican friends and their families: calling them derogatory names like "Spics," "Cholos," or "Beaners." This bothered me and left me confused. I became aware that the town where I lived was almost totally white, except for the Mexicans who comprised most of its lower classes. They usually lived in their barrios, some in town, and some out near the groves.

It was at Sycamore Junior High that my ninth-grade English teacher, Mr. Beach, gave the class an assignment to choose a book to give a report on. This assignment changed my life. I randomly chose, *The Call of The Wild* by Jack London. This short adventure story is about a Yukon sled dog's struggle to survive under brutal conditions during the Alaskan gold rush of the 1890s. When it was published in 1903, it became enormously popular, and eventually was considered one of American literature's greatest stories. It also established Jack London as one of the most popular writers in America. The *Call of the Wild* led me to read other works of his.

At the time, I didn't know who Jack London was, let alone that, in his day, he'd been a well-known socialist, a member of the US Communist Party, and an ardent critic of the American capitalistic political/economic system. These were ideas I had never even thought about. Growing up in the San Francisco/Oakland Bay area, Jack London was the son of a poor, working-class family. Self-educated, his socialist views didn't develop from an academic or philosophical study but grew out of his experiences growing up into a harsh, yet beautiful world.

London was an adventurer who travelled the globe as a sailor on tramp steamers and lived out on the road, traveling as a vagrant in railroad boxcars with hobos. Because he had no fixed address, and no visible means of support, the cop's hand-cuffed him, chained him to a bunch of men of similar circumstance and sent him off to a county penitentiary where he wore jail stripes and did hard time. Experiencing life from the bottom up, he described the condition within which most of humanity exists, as a walled in "Social Pit": a place that he had slipped into; a place where once a man slipped down into, there was little chance of ever rising above it. Through his own strength of character and will, he eventually climbed out of the Social Pit, to become one of the world's most prominent writers.

After reading *The Call of the Wild* and other adventure tales, I read other books of his that opened up a world unlike my own. It was through Jack London's writing that I, at a young age, began to understand the world around me. He wrote about the unfair and brutal nature of the economic system we live under, known as capitalism. He explained concepts and words like "Class," "Class-Consciousness," "Aristocracy" and "Oligarchy," "Bourgeoisie" and "Proletarian." He wrote for the average person. He wrote to explain to us how we live, in a class-divided society, ruled by a wealthy elite class that is always taking for itself, and working against the interests of the common people. He wrote about the world in a way I could relate to because my family was also working-class, and I had, within the past few years, observed a few instances of the kinds of injustices about which he wrote.

My sister Becky, five years older than I also became another major influence on my thinking during this time and helped give me an understanding of what was going on in the world. She had been an excellent student in high school and achieved a partial scholarship and acceptance to study at San Jose State, a college up north in the bay area. When she would come home on the holidays and semester breaks, we would talk for hours about the things she was learning; things that seemed so completely different from what I'd always been taught. Majoring in sociology, she had been introduced to an entirely different world, perceived through academic rational inquiry, and scientific method. This contrasted with the blind, dogmatic, bigoted world I had been raised to accept as reality. Becky was a beacon of light, a "Marco Polo," of sorts, coming home to share the news of what she'd learned. She carried with her a novel way of thinking about things way beyond the provincial ignorance of all that I knew. She spoke about things like prejudice, bigotry, racism, and social injustice, and it was through our discussions that I came to understand that many people, because of cultural and religious intolerance, believed they were superior to others. I realized it was this mentality that explained why the Mexicans in Anaheim lived separately, on dirt roads, in barrio shanties, while white people lived in our tract homes with nicely trimmed and manicured lawns. In America, I realized, the class system was set up so some seem to have it all while so many have nothing.

CHAPTER 2

The Summer of 1963

IT WAS ON a hot summer night in 1963 when I first became aware of a country called Vietnam.

I was fifteen years old, having the best summer of my life. Newport Beach, 15th Street, was our favorite spot, a perfect sandy beach where the surf would just keep rolling in wave after wave, great for body surfing. We didn't have a care in the world. My friends and I would spend our days on the beach, and in the evenings go to Disneyland or other hot-spot places to dance and rock-out with our girlfriends to the bands and entertainment all around us. It was an incredible time. I was a white surfer boy growing up in Orange County, Southern California.

I wasn't a Sosh or a Greaser, I was a Surfer. A surfer was a different social class. The Sosh's were the school phonies; those kids who wanted to be popular with everybody, especially the teachers. They were the kiss-ass student leaders, the student body shits. The Greasers were the punks who wanted to project a James Dean look with their jelly roll haircuts and anti-authoritarian attitudes. Surfers were different. We were laid back.

We were the lifestyle that the Beach Boys sang about,

And they're out there having fun,
in that warm California sun

What more could a fifteen-year-old ask for? My friends and I were on top of the world, and we knew it. Media and music popularized and played up our Southern California surfing youth culture to the hilt. The myth of our self-made paradise played non-stop on radio and TV, in movies like *Gidget.* We lived it and we believed it was real. It was paradise.

I'd been down at the beach all day body surfing and hanging out with my school friends on the sand. Around 4 o'clock, I picked up my beach towel and made my way home in the usual way. I hitched rides for the twenty miles up Harbor Boulevard through Costa Mesa and into Santa Ana, and then to Anaheim and my family home. After dinner, my family sat down in the living room to watch the evening news, featuring Walter Cronkite. As the broadcast began, Walter explained that what we were going to see that night was something different from what we usually watched, and it could be disturbing. We didn't look away from the screen. I saw it.

Naive and simplistic shows like *Leave it To Beaver, Father Knows Best* or *The Beverly Hillbillies,* were the shows we watched. The most violent things that we would have watched in those TV days, were scenes out of the popular western series about life and frontier justice in the Old West, *Gunsmoke.*

So, it was a strange and unexpected thing to see the broadcast that evening, something so real and violent. A young Buddhist monk, wearing robes, got out of his car and calmly walked to the center of a crowded city traffic circle where he knelt down, straightened his back, and lit a match. He burst into flames instantly, burning like a human torch for all of us and the world to see. It was called a *self-immolation*. The Buddhist monks who surrounded him began chanting something as the crowd went wildly out of control. The Vietnamese military police reacted by firing their guns into the crowd. These horrifying acts of violence we observed in our living rooms that evening were something that had far-reaching emotional consequences. I had seen nothing like this before and I felt its emotional impact immediately. The entire world saw it. I remember being very upset by what I had seen, wanting to understand what it was all about. The image from that night pushed out any remaining joy from my carefree afternoon at the beach. But that was just one summer evening that I soon forgot.

|||

With September came the end of summer vacation. My time at Sycamore Junior High had been filled with success – athletic and artistic – and good times. Anaheim High School was a different story. It felt like a prison to me. Its campus, with a student body of over twenty-five hundred, was a place I knew I'd become just a number. There was something about that school that repulsed me, but I didn't really understand my feelings. It just felt uncomfortable. It was the original high school in Anaheim, founded shortly after German colonists settled the town back in 1857. It had rigid traditions and an exclusive social structure solidified over the decades into a deadened place. If a guy coming in from the outside was going to be anyone at Anaheim High, he had to make it on the football team, student government, academics, or into the various clubs and I wasn't into any of it.

Before school began that year I received a letter from the Anaheim High School football coaching staff inviting me to join the sophomore training camp to get ready for the up-and-coming football season. Even though the Anaheim High football team was one of the most highly regarded football teams in the state of California, and I really loved playing football, I passed on the opportunity without a second thought. The choice was simple. Which would I rather do: go surfing and hang out on the beach every day with all the beautiful chicks, or report to the summer football camp where I would be forced to do wind sprints in the heavy Southern California smog, until I barfed? Simple choice. I got through the experience of Anaheim High School somehow by doing as little as I could while still enjoying my social life on the outside, which had nothing to do with school. I decided not to be a football hero, and I was happy with being a nobody. I mostly ignored those students who wanted to be part of the Anaheim High School experience and hung out with kids who felt the same way I did. We were the outsiders and we liked it.

| | |

It was November. I was at school, sitting in my chair in the art classroom working on a portrait of another art student when I noticed the commotion. The art teacher from the classroom next door had come into our classroom and begun, in a hushed and serious tone, talking with my art teacher about something. They were standing right behind me talking and I picked up on their words. The kids in the class picked up on it too. After a while, the school principal came on the intercom to announce to us the very disturbing news that was being reported. Someone had shot the President of the United States! After a tense period, sitting in our classrooms, maybe a half hour later, the principal came back on to tell us somberly that the President of the United States was dead. An assassin had killed President John F. Kennedy.

When the period break bell sounded, I went out into the crowded locker hallways and watched as near hysteria broke out amongst the students. Many cried in disbelief. When the bell sounded for lunch break to begin, most of us left school and went home to watch the developing story on TV. The very real film images of the President's brains being splattered were too much for us to handle.

November 22, 1963 was a horrible day.

CHAPTER 3

Questioning Things

THROUGHOUT THE SIXTIES, Mom and Dad subscribed to *Life Magazine* and other popular publications reporting on current events both here in the US and around the world. The reporting and the black and white photography were excellent, and through these magazines, newspapers, and other sources, I gained an understanding of current events. At age fourteen, I found myself sitting on the floor at the coffee table, glancing through these magazines, contemplating the meaning of it all.

During this time, I began to pay attention to political events that were happening right here where I lived in Orange County. I learned that Orange County was a bastion of not just conservative Republican politics, but way out, to the extreme right, of politics. It is where Richard Milhous Nixon, who became a legendary virulent anti-communist, was born and raised on an orange farm, near Anaheim. The ultra-right-wing John Birch Society was very comfortable here and considered Orange County to be their home base. After studying for a while, I concluded that my overwhelmingly white hometown of Anaheim was a town of racism. An extreme fear and hatred of "communism" united them. They felt that communism was the most dangerous and evil thing in the world and they would fight to the death to destroy it. Communism was their over-riding concern.

I was living behind something that later became infamously known around the country as the "Orange Curtain". Orange County's extreme anti-communism was a big deal, and I realized these bigoted, racist, and anti-communist ideals were all tied in with each other. This mind-set, so prevalent in the people of my community didn't sit well with me. My studies, beginning with the books I'd read by Jack London left me understanding that a socialist economy would be a far better way to organize society than the cruel, dog-eat-dog capitalist economy under which we all lived and suffered. I was a socialist living in an extreme, right-wing, anti-communist and anti-socialist world, and I realized then that I didn't fit in. I was living as an outsider in my own community. With the civil rights struggle led by Martin Luther King, Jr. and the horrific war in Vietnam being broadcast on television every night, I questioned our country and everything it was built upon. The horrific sight of the Buddhist monk burning himself alive came back to me time and time again. After the Kennedy assassination, my thoughts and feelings about our nation's economic and political system came together; its racist and brutal ways made it difficult for me to accept any of it.

My decision to not go out for football and to become a nobody at Anaheim High proved to be the right move. The school was a miserable waste of time. Administered by a school board rigidly controlled by an extreme right-wing political and religious ideology, it did nothing but reflect the warped values of its societal context. Much of our education was nothing more than poorly-veiled propaganda intended to indoctrinate us into a conformist, blind submission to these values. I felt terrible about this because I really did like so many of the kids at the school who just couldn't see and understand things as I did.

Anaheim High Senior Picture
Class of 1966

Even though the school seemed like a prison,
I found other ways during those years to enjoy life.

Nixon

*Richard Milhous Nixon, the 37ᵗʰ United States President,
built his political career on virulent anti-communism.*

*He was born and raised on an orange farm, not
far from where I grew up in Anaheim.*

CHAPTER 4

The Draft

SINCE 1917, ALL young men in America, upon reaching the age of eighteen, were required by law to register with the country's "Selective Service Board," better known as the "Draft Board." They ordered us to report to induction centers across the nation where they would inspect us to determine if we were healthy enough, both physically and mentally, to be drafted into the United States Armed Forces. After high school graduation, in the summer of my eighteenth year, I received a letter from the draft board ordering me to report for my pre-induction physical examination. The letter included a warning that my failure to report for the examination would be a Federal crime punishable by law. It commanded me to get on an early morning bus at a local station, which would take me to the downtown Los Angeles Selective Service Induction Center for my examination.

The Los Angeles Pre-Induction Center Physical experience was an unbelievable psychological horror show. We were just kids delivered on a bus to this seedy, old twelve-story building, in the Skid Row district of downtown Los Angeles. They ordered us to strip and stand all day in long lines in nothing but our underwear, where uniformed military staff threatened and abused us. They were complete assholes; wearing their Army and Marine Corps uniforms, bossing us around and issuing insulting commands to us like,

"Bend over and grab your ankles, girls."

I recall being in a line to have my blood drawn. Standing there in the filthiest of conditions, we were being shouted at to move up so that poorly trained medics could stick needles into our arms while they laughed and yelled,

"Get up here you little wimp, I'm gonna stick you."

I saw a few guys pass out from the sight of their own blood dripping on the floor.

It was the most degrading experience imaginable, and it left us with a taste of what it might be like if we were drafted. They also collected lots of information from us, which they needed to more efficiently suck us up into their current war; the Vietnam War, which few of us even believed in. We had no rights.

College offered a way out. The Selective Service Board allowed college deferments which could delay induction into the military. If you enrolled in a college program and took at least twelve college units each semester, you might qualify to get a school deferment. And so, I enrolled at my local community school, Fullerton Junior College. I found I liked college. The professors, teachers, and the intellectual activities at FJC were a far better experience from what I'd had in high school. I'd barely graduated from Anaheim High, but that was because it was such a depressing, ignorant school; seventy percent of its faculty were also part-time athletic coaches. Despite my miserable high school record, my college entrance exam scores enabled me to enter my freshman college year without having to take any remedial, or dumbbell classes. The FJC campus was alive with new ideas and creative energy, an environment I loved.

Lots of things were being discussed in my classes at Fullerton Junior College in the fall of 1966, and the Vietnam

War was front and center. "Teach-ins" were being held on college campuses all over the country, intending to educate, analyze, and discuss the pros and cons of the war. I attended a few of these teach-ins at FJC and read the history of Vietnam and many books that dealt with the political events which had led us into the war. As I studied, I became increasingly against the war for several reasons: It was unnecessary; the people of Vietnam and their country were not attacking us, nor did they pose a threat to any other nation; The people of Vietnam only wanted their independence and to be left alone, to be able to settle their affairs without interference from outside forces; The United States had seriously interfered with, and made sure that free and open Democratic elections would never happen, which led to the installation of an illegitimate South Vietnamese government led by America's chosen puppets; The Vietnam War was "unwinnable" because the South Vietnamese government, along with its officials and senior military commanders, whom the United States had forcefully installed upon the people of Vietnam, were appallingly corrupt and incompetent. What America was engaging in was a disaster in the making.

Most of the students attending these teach-ins became as against the war as I was. College students across the country were waking up to the folly of it all and a rebellion was rapidly growing. Young men were increasingly becoming aware that this was a war being conducted by old white men; political relics, we saw as corrupt.

We rebelled against the "system" – a system which had the authority to order us, after reaching the age of eighteen, to report to the country for military induction into their criminal, genocidal war. We resisted those who would place our names on lists and threaten us with arrest if we did not go along with their program. It was that simple. The FBI would come looking for you, even at your parents' house, if you did so.

It became a war of us against them.

Corrupt Politicians

The war made no sense to most of us young guys who were threatened by the draft. It was a war being conducted by old white men we saw as relics.

CHAPTER 5

The Generation Gap

DAD WAS A proud World War II Navy veteran. He'd served in the South Pacific War, fighting against the Japanese Empire which had aligned with Hitler and his Nazis in the Axis fascist empire attempting to take over the world. The Pacific War was an extremely violent war where American forces suffered enormous losses of over one hundred thousand.

A tough working class "Okie," Dad had grown up during the Great Depression and the Dust Bowl in Oklahoma. He was a hard-working, hard-drinking, patriotic, red-neck kind of guy through and through, who had no tolerance for weaklings or those who had been coined "draft dodgers." He was straight out of the "Silent Generation"; those who would do whatever their county asked of them, right or wrong, quietly and without question. His father had grown up as a cowboy out in the Old West on the plains of Kansas, where the only law was through the barrel of a gun. His grandfather had fought with the Union Army in the Civil War. Dad's great-grandfather rode with the Texas Rangers and was one of the first fighters to enter the Mexican-American war under General Zachary Taylor. Well before that, the Gibson men fought in the

Indian Wars and the Revolutionary War before that. War was ingrained in my family's DNA.

Like so many men of his generation, Dad couldn't understand where in the hell I and so many of my generation were coming from questioning and resisting the Vietnam War. It was not the American way. It was not patriotic. This was because America, in his eyes, was always the good guy in any conflict. Living in his house was sometimes intolerable. He would hound me about what he considered my lack of patriotism. Occasionally he called me a communist or a cowardly traitor because of my objections to the war. Dad was always in my face about either getting a job and paying him room and board, or just going into the military. He would not tolerate any "loafers" in his house and wanted me to grow up and face the real world. He wanted me to become what he considered to be a man.

My generation, which would become known as the "Baby Boomer" generation, had developed a mindset that was very different from that of our parents. We didn't mindlessly accept things and we were into questioning everything. We even had a slogan: "Question Authority."

"Trip" (Damon Evans Walk III) represented the greatest contrast in generational values of anyone I knew. He was an outrageous kid who did whatever he wanted to do all the time, regardless of the consequences, and I loved him because of it. One day he invited me to join him with a few girlfriends to go up into the local mountains and smoke marijuana. I hadn't smoked before, but I knew that he and several of my friends were into it, so I agreed to go. We took off in his Volkswagen Beetle that afternoon with his eight-track stereo blaring at maximum volume all the way up into the mountains. After a while, we got off the paved road, and took a rutted dirt road to an isolated and beautiful spot known appropriately as "Holy Jim Canyon." With Trip and a beautiful young hippie girlfriend, Janis, we lit up a carefully wrapped joint. I inhaled the smoke for the first time and right away entered a whole new and pleasurable world. We all got stoned –"ripped," as we said during that time. We laughed and frolicked, tumbling down the canyon hillsides in the grass together. For hours, this went on, smoking joint after joint, until after dark. After a while we pulled ourselves together and drove back down the mountain, returning to our homes for school the next day. I loved the experience and started smoking pot regularly. Of course, I hid this entirely from my parents, who would have thought I'd gone insane.

CHAPTER 6

Spiritual and Political Things

BEGINNING IN THE mid-sixties, the Hippie "Love, Peace, and Anti-war" counter-cultural thing became huge, with its anti-establishment messages of "Flower Power," and "Make Love Not War." I became utterly fascinated with it all. It was all about people peacefully, nonviolently, living together spiritually — a world of peace and love as opposed to war and violence. It felt so natural to me that it seemed I was born with this consciousness.

Trip was an advocate of the psychedelic drug lysergic acid diethylamide, LSD. He would go on and on about the incredible spiritual revelations that he experienced on his acid trips. He explained to me that taking LSD was not a partying thing; it was nothing like the drinking and partying we had done so much of in high school. He said that these psychedelic journeys had taught him much about the underlying truths of life. Those who were into it spoke of their experiences as if entering through "The Doors of Perception." It all seemed so spiritually peaceful and loving. There were several friends I was hanging out with in and around Anaheim in those days who were also very much into the acid scene.

Dropping acid was commonplace by then. One night, Trip helped my friend Randy and me score a hit of acid. We split it, swallowed it, and drove down to Scotchman's Cove, an inlet just north of Laguna Beach to have our nature experience on the beach. We walked down a dirt path to the surf and the water's edge and watched the incredible things going on there along the moonlit, phosphorescent ocean sand. It was a beautiful and peaceful experience. So magical. I had never seen or experienced anything as beautiful as that before.

On another Saturday morning, Randy and I split another tab of acid and spent the entire day, a beautiful sunny day, stoned out of our minds, roaming the Balboa Beach Peninsula. When I returned home later in the day, I was pretty much peeking out on the acid when I found myself in a conversation with the next-door neighbor girl. I recall I felt I could read her mind and knew before she said a word exactly what she was going to say. This left me with the undeniable feeling that I could see through and understand everything. This acid trip was amazing. It was everything I had heard it could be. *Everything was so beautiful.*

Later that evening, Randy and I went to see Jefferson Airplane in concert at our local convention center arena in Anaheim. Their opening act was The Doors. There were thousands of young people there just like us in the convention center, seemingly just as stoned out of their minds as we were. This was the Hippie time. It was the Freak time. It was like we were all on this same incredible acid trip together. We were turned on, we were on the loose, and we were going to take over. We were the Long Hairs and Revolution was in the air! Seeing The Jefferson Airplane and The Doors was a mind-blowing experience to top off an unbelievable day.

We were tripping out for sure, rejecting the direction of the past which we knew we had to change. The headlining group, Jefferson Airplane, from San Francisco was the first psychedelic rock band to achieve international success in that genre. They had just released their album *Surrealistic Pillow* which included the songs "Somebody to Love" and "White Rabbit." The Doors followed them with renditions of "Light My Fire" and "The End."

The arena crowd was on fire that night with the spirit of it all and the heavy smell of marijuana wafting throughout the auditorium. The Anaheim police were not happy with it at all. They hung out in the wings of the stage that night hoping to catch a glimpse of the lead singer of the Doors, Jim Morrison, getting a blow job, so they could arrest him. Cops all over the country were trying to nail Jim in whatever way they could and had passed along this completely false and slanderous narrative of his sexual immorality from department to department. The feeling of disconnect between the police and the young people in the crowd pervaded everything. We called them Pigs because they acted like pigs.

It seemed I could see for miles and miles. I recall the Love-Ins in Griffith Park in Los Angeles, and in Irvine Park in Orange County. These were communal events where thousands would show up in the parks, getting high on LSD and other psychedelic drugs, partying and listening to the most popular music groups playing for free. It was all FREE. I saw generations of families, parents, children and grandchildren, wearing headbands with flowers in their hair, dropping acid together, swaying to the music on the grassy hillsides in the park, where you might see couples openly having sex together in complete and total freedom. There has never been a time like that before or since.

America was really tripping out.

There was something going on in south Orange County, in Laguna Beach. An LSD-inspired group of hippies, some of them connected to old friends of mine from Anaheim, like Trip, had come together and legally incorporated themselves into something known as the Brotherhood of Eternal Love. The Brotherhood had a mission of spreading the love and understanding and "cosmic consciousness," which they felt that they had discovered through their use of psychedelic drugs. Their mission was to share and spread this spiritual consciousness to the world as dealers of these illegal substances. I believe that they were mostly sincere but also into making lots of money while doing so. There were just a few characters who made up the core of the Brotherhood, a secretive, exclusive, organization. Their legend spread quickly through the psychedelic underground in Orange County. The famous media psychedelic psychologist of the time, Timothy Leary, who became known as the "Guru of LSD," with his message of "Turn on, tune in, and Drop Out," somehow found out about The Brotherhood, and linked up with them.

He moved with his family to Laguna Beach and settled into a house in Laguna Canyon. The Brotherhood became a big-time organization, involved with producing and selling tens of thousands of hits of LSD, such as "Orange Sunshine", while also smuggling and supplying tons of hashish to America. Timothy Leary would sometimes hold meditative "acid court" in an exclusive back room of a Laguna Beach book and gift shop front, located right there on Pacific Coast Highway, known as "The Mystic Arts." This was an incredibly crafted place, carpeted with expensive Persian rugs, handcrafted by the hippie carpenters and artisans of Laguna Beach who had for so many years populated and created their art there.

My friends and I would get together privately most

evenings in homes with the heavy smell of incense and marijuana burning, get stoned, have our experiences, and listen to LP vinyl records playing the great music of that era. I loved it. We were into the music and the alternative lifestyle; we questioned and rejected much of what our parents had taught us. Established cultural and religious consciousness was rapidly being scorned and reformed by our youth culture. I studied eastern religions and read the Egyptian Book of the Dead, the *Bhagavad Gita*, among other texts of religions and beliefs.

While having these spiritual experiences, I was also taking part and involved in political activism. I attended many of the local anti-war meetings which were being held in private homes near Fullerton Junior College during the spring semester of 1967. I also connected with a larger group of student activists who had been organizing on the campus of the newly established University of California at Irvine, UCI. This group became known as, "The Orange County Committee Against the War in Vietnam." This excited me at first and I attended their meetings for a while with great hope, but in time found that I felt uncomfortable being there. I was into a political change brought through the elevation of a consciousness of peace, love, and nonviolence. I felt it was through this kind of spiritual change, advocated by the great leaders, Dr. Martin Luther King, Jr., and Mahatma Gandhi, that genuine change would come about. It had to come about through a combination of loving spiritual and political energy.

I was having a hard time reconciling my spiritual feelings with the anti-war political types who seemed intent on promoting a kind of old-style political leftist ideology that included violent anti-war resistance. I stopped attending their meetings because I sensed hidden agendas. I had been attempting to blend these two worlds of the spiritual and the political, but they were incompatible. The political and the spiritual didn't see things in the same way. There were few of my friends during that time who cared about either one of these things that I cared about. Most of them weren't as serious as I was and could give a flying fuck about the spiritual or the political. They were mostly into getting out of their frightening realities in whatever ways they could, usually escaping through music, sex, and drugs.

After my second semester at Fullerton Junior college, I was having trouble focusing and drifted. My grades were so bad they put me on academic probation. I enrolled for the following fall semester but couldn't get back into studying and started missing classes. I then dropped out of college altogether, got a job in a local factory, rented an apartment, and moved out of my father's house. When I dropped out, the college immediately notified the draft board who, shortly thereafter, sent me a letter stating that I had lost my college deferment and was ready to be drafted.

My love affair with LSD crashed and burned on July 4, 1967. That morning I met with a few friends in the back of a VW bus in a city park in Anaheim, where we split and shared capsules of LSD then a cruise down to Newport Beach. The "Bum Trip" was about to begin. After about twenty minutes, as we were crossing the Newport Bay Bridge, I noticed things were changing in extraordinary ways that I had never experienced before. Suddenly I felt as though I was completely lost. Panic set in as I felt that I did not know where I was or what was happening to me. That acid trip turned out to be a horrible experience, and I was glad when I could finally come down from it and the experience was over. It took me nearly twelve horrible. hours to come down. I have experienced nothing as frightening as that experience, before or since. I swore it off.

I turned away; turned inward, to separate and shield myself from the madness that I saw and felt all around me. I had learned a lot from my political experiences, my psychedelic experiences, my religious studies, and meditation. These studies and experiences revealed that what I was going through was a spiritual thing; Everything is an illusion, an expression of the temporal, dualistic world of ever-changing things. The lesson was that you just had to hang on with or without cosmic consciousness.

III

It was in the fall of 1967 when I found myself living unhappily in an apartment in Anaheim, sharing it with a roommate. We smoked pot together often and sometimes took the speed pills known then as "Bennies." He was a childhood friend of mine whom I became convinced had become completely psycho. I had to get away from him. I also was disgusted with the menial job I was working at in Fullerton, a ball bearing machine shop. I quit my job, then, without the means to live on, and wanting to get out of my situation, approached my dad and asked him if I could live at home again. I told him I would get another job and pay him room and board, and he accepted my request. I got a job in another factory and began a different chapter in my life. I had been turned off to the hippie drug scene and the anti-war movement political scene by then, so I just bade my time for a while. I stopped smoking Marijuana and taking drugs entirely.

"Transcendental Meditation" was the creation of an Indian Guru by the name of Maharishi Mahesh Yogi, whom the Beatles and other famous Hollywood personalities had discovered and made the rage. They had become enamored with him and travelled to India to study and master his technique of salvation, which promised to render peace and love and harmony without having to rely on the crutch of drugs or anything else. He would accomplish all of this through his secret technical practice of "Transcendental Meditation" (TM).

I was 19 years old in February 1968, when I became interested in TM and was initiated into its practice. Meditating TM twice daily in my darkened bedroom closet for thirty minutes in the morning before work, and thirty minutes after work every day. The practice had a calming and settling effect on my life during that time. I was out of the drug scene, out of the political scene, and just wanted to be alone in peace. So, I pretty much cut off most of my friends and my social life. I was biding my time and waiting for the inevitable draft notice to come. I didn't know what I was going to do. Everything seemed hopeless, but the meditation helped in some ways.

My twentieth birthday, March 24, 1968, came and went. Exactly eleven days later on April 4, in Memphis, Tennessee, Dr. Martin Luther King, Jr. was shot and killed. Social turmoil unfolded, pitting not just Blacks against whites but unleashing many other pent up social tensions that had been simmering for many years. There was a lot of awakening during this time to the existence of class differentiation. A social consciousness was rising about those who have and those who have not. Women were demanding their rights. Gays rose up against their persecution. People were fed up with "The System", a system of inequality. Revolution was in the air. Resistance to the Vietnam war in America during this time had gotten to where student radicals bombed draft office buildings and set fire to banks all around the country. Many of America's cities were on fire, out of control and burning. The rage was a spectacle for all to behold on the nightly news with the grim newsreels of death and horrible, brutal, destruction being carried out by US soldiers in Vietnam. We were murdering innocent peasants there on a mass scale.

Yet even though there was so much evidence of this atrocity, the American public was effectively being misled and manipulated by politicians like Richard Nixon, who created and labelled something that he called "The Silent Majority." These were the so called "True Patriotic Americans." They were the Silent Generation— those who stood by while their government, right or wrong continued its genocidal slaughter of hundreds of thousands of innocent Vietnamese people. Many who identified with the "Silent Majority" were white racist Christian types, who mercilessly condemned the "Niggers," "Jews", and the other minorities. They condemned the "Anti-Americans", and the "Communists; the atheists, and all of those 'Hippie Pukes' (that was me) the long hairs, whom they considered degenerates. Often police officers, preachers of Law and Order, arrested us without cause. Sometimes they were construction workers with hard hats who wrapped themselves up in American flags and beat the anti-war protestors with baseball bats; their favorite expression to those of us who were protesting the war and the crimes of our country was "Love it or leave it".

Sadly, and to my dismay, my father and my older Brother, JC, considered themselves to be part of this silent majority. The TV scenes of America's cities on fire, the result of our nation's deeply embedded racism, along with the scenes of Vietnam villages being torched and burned to the ground, were unbearable. That so many American people, including my father and my brother, were seemingly untouched by this unnecessary violence, seared into my consciousness with the message that much of my country was insane; it was something I wanted no part of. I had to keep reminding myself: what I was going through was a spiritual thing: everything is an illusion, an expression of the temporal, dualistic, world of the ever-changing things. The lesson was that you just had to hang on with or without cosmic consciousness.

In those days when our country was seeing hundreds dead and thousands wounded every week on the battlefields in Vietnam, there was an enormous need for replacements. The call-ups of draftees sometimes numbered in the tens of thousands every month. Sometimes sixty or seventy thousand young men would get their draft notices in a single month. I knew it would not be long before I would get my own notice, so I pondered on what I was going to do to get out of this shit. I was biding my time, working at a meaningless job, waiting around. They were coming to get me.

Even though I had entertained the alternative worlds of spiritual awareness and consciousness, I still felt a strong desire to do something positive in the everyday, temporal, political world unfolding around me. I followed the news religiously and could see serious efforts were still being made by many Democrats to get us out of the Vietnam War.

There was an anti-war candidate running for President in the upcoming election of 1968 who ran on the promise to do just that. The "Peace Candidate," Senator Eugene McCarthy of Minnesota, seemed far different from the other Democratic politicians. He became known as "Clean Gene." I went out on several afternoons during this time, door-to-door precinct walking for Eugene McCarthy with my older sister Becky accompanying me. Becky was, like me, very much opposed to the war. We handed out McCarthy campaign literature and spoke with neighborhood residents.

I could tell my time before being drafted was growing short. I was reading and watching the news reports: tens of thousands of young men across America were being called up by the draft and I figured correctly that I would receive my letter from the President of the United States ordering me to report for induction soon. The Draft Board seemed to draft recruits in order, alphabetically, and the news reported that they were then drafting those whose last names started with D. I calculated and could discern from this that the "G's" (my last name Gibson) would most likely get their induction notices in or around early June 1968.

Even though I had left behind the psychedelic world I had become burned out with, I still maintained friendships with others who were into it. Gerry, a close friend of mine, had connections with the Brotherhood dealers down in Laguna Beach with their mission of turning on the world to peace and love through their dealings. He was part of their secretive inner circle and quite a dealer of psychedelics himself.

Gerry and his wife Ginny were true hippies. They dealt LSD and other psychedelics in large quantities and made a comfortable living from their home where they lived inconspicuous lives in an old house on a quiet street, in a tree-shaded neighborhood in old Fullerton. They tried to stay out of sight and did. They always welcomed me into their warm, dimly lit, gypsy-like home, where I spent many enjoyable evenings with them and other friends, listening to music in contemplation and conversation of the worldly and spiritual events happening around us. It was all about gaining in spiritual awareness, and I loved the evenings spent with them.

Steve, an old friend of mine whom I had known since

Junior High days, was a regular at Gerry and Ginny's place. He was not only against the war in Vietnam, as we all were, but was absolutely freaked out by the prospect of being drafted. We both faced this dilemma together, and we were certain they would draft us around the same time in June. This was because our last names both started with the letter G.

Gerry didn't have to worry about the draft because of a physical injury that gave him a permanent disability deferment, but Steve and I were both deemed physically fit by the draft board and stamped as prime beef for the slaughter. The three of us spent many contemplative evenings pondering different ways that Steve and I might somehow get out of it. I decided that my best bet was to make a run for it; to escape across the border into Canada. Gerry, who had been a world traveler and adventurer, offered me his backpack and anything else he had that I might need to make my journey. Steve was always an insecure kid, and couldn't handle the prospect of doing something so drastic.

The war in Vietnam continued to dominate the news with weekly reports of American casualties. A friend of mine told me there was going to be a going-away party for a kid in our neighborhood we'd grown up with—Rodney. He was on leave from the Army, waiting shipment off to Vietnam. I didn't know Rodney very well, but he always seemed like a shy, likeable kind of guy. We got together at someone's apartment that night, got loose drinking lots of beer, and wished Rodney well before his departure, which was to occur the next morning. He told us all proudly they had trained him as an Army combat medic, and he was looking forward very much to going to the war to help save the lives of his fellow soldiers.

Not long after, we got the sad news that Rodney was dead. He had been killed less than two weeks after his arrival in

Vietnam. Along with this news, there were also stories going around about what other school friends who had gone to Vietnam had experienced. These were the most horrifying tales I had ever heard. You can't imagine how grisly they were.

CHAPTER 7

Drastic Measures

THE NEWS OF Rodney's death combined with the war stories that were getting back to us from Vietnam convinced us we had to find a way out of it. Gerry, Steve, and I continued to meet and think about what we were going to do. My plan was to hitchhike to Canada to escape the war as many young American men had chosen to do. Steve was too timid to try anything like that. He looked at Gerry with his permanent disqualifying disability and decided he too should try to become physically disabled.

Gerry and Steve came up with a plan to get Steve out of the draft by breaking his arm. This would get him a deferment. The most drastic of times were upon us, and they would require drastic measures. We knew it wouldn't be long before we would get our draft notices, and then after failing to appear, the government would come looking for us. I got my backpack and things ready to hit the road to Canada while the three of us conjured up what we thought was an almost foolproof way to break Steve's arm.

It was a Sunday afternoon when we helped Steve get stoned on pain pills to the point of nearly passing out. We then brought him out to Gerry's garage, where we had set up two concrete cinder blocks on a table, spaced about eight inches apart. Steve sat down on a chair and carefully rested his right forearm down on the blocks. Gerry took out a heavy, solid steel dumbbell bar. Steve braced himself as Gerry stood up, raising the rod high over his head with both hands. He then chanted out something that seemed very all forgiving and transcendent. An intense second elapsed before Gerry came crashing down with all his might on Steve's arm.

Wham!

Steve gasped...

"Ugh... ugh... ugh..."

Gerry and I looked at each other. There was a problem. We hadn't been successful. There was no snapping or breaking sound, nor any visible evidence that we had succeeded. With Steve moaning, Gerry stood one more time and came down again on it. That didn't work either. So, after a few more tries without success, he handed the dumbbell bar to me and I stood up and wailed away a few more times on Steve's arm myself, with all my might.

The bone remained unbroken!

By this time, we could see that Steve's arm was rapidly swelling and changing into a horrible shade of red purple as he gasped, cried out, and moaned in horrific pain. The pre-plan was to break Steve's arm, then rush him immediately to the local Emergency Room at Martin Luther Hospital, just a few miles away in Anaheim. We knew beforehand that Gerry's mom, who knew Steve well, would be the acting head ER nurse in charge that day. She had absolutely no knowledge of what we were up to. Within twenty minutes, we brought Steve into the ER, where Gerry's mom greeted us with immense concern at the entrance and immediately cared for him. After they rushed Steve off to get x-rayed, she asked us what in the world had happened to him. According to our made-up plan, we explained we had been working on a car in Gerry's garage when it had come loose from its jacks and crashed down on Steve's arm. She bought the story.

While Gerry and I were waiting around in the ER for word on the exam of Steve's arm, a very synchronistic event occurred which brings us back to something I mentioned earlier—

"Life takes us into the unexpected where we begin our journeys into the unknown with small steps into what lies ahead, usually without awareness of the things that have influenced us."

Gerry and I were sitting there on that quiet Sunday in the Emergency Room waiting for the results of Steve's examination when, unannounced, an ambulance pulled up. They brought in a gurney with a young man who had horrible, life-threatening, bloody injuries, the result of a motorcycle accident. Gerry's Mom who was working by herself in the ER that day needed to transfer him off the ambulance's gurney and onto the hospital's but there was no one there to help her do this so she yelled out to Gerry and me. Gerry couldn't bring himself to deal with this and refrained, but I immediately rose and helped her transfer him. The kid was dripping in blood when I, without hesitation, stepped in to help with my own two hands.

|||

Gerry and I waited around for a long time for Steve to come out, but I needed to go home and prepare for my escape to Canada. I knew Steve was now in safe hands and going to be alright, so I left the hospital. I learned later that the boy in the motorcycle accident died from his injuries. The experience left me understanding that I could deal with this kind of extreme medical situation without freaking out – an ability I had - that would later prove especially useful.

I told my Dad that evening what I was up to and he seemed to understand. My plan was to hitchhike north to Canada, but in the beginning I was going to take a Greyhound Bus from the Anaheim depot to San Luis Obispo before hitchhiking north. He offered to take me to the bus station in the morning and I took him up on his offer.

CHAPTER EIGHT

The Road North

I AWOKE EARLY and prepared my backpack and other supplies. I think all I had at the time in my wallet was about a hundred and fifty dollars, my total worth. Dad drove me to the Greyhound bus station where he dropped me off and gave me a serious look and a bit of warning advice: "Be careful of those who you meet and travel with out there on the road."

The Anaheim bus station was located just a stone's throw from the sunny front gate of the "Happiest Place on Earth," Disneyland. The first stop was the central Los Angeles bus terminal which was in the heart of downtown LA's skid row. From the happiest place on earth, the bus had transported me in a matter of a few hours, to what looked like the Unhappiest Place on Earth. What a weird, scary, filthy fucking place that Greyhound bus station was. A place I wanted to get away from for sure. From there I rode the Greyhound north through Santa Barbara and all the other small towns along the central California coast, for about 200 miles until I got off the bus in the city of San Luis Obispo. This was where I would begin my hitchhiking journey.

In the spring of 1968, lots of young people were taking off and hitchhiking across America. We were hippies, out there on the road with nothing but our long hair, beads, beards, backpacks and sleeping bags, just escaping things and being free. This was the sixties in all its heyday when many of the kids of our generation were getting stoned so much of the time, mostly on pot and acid and other psychedelics. I was out of the drug scene by this time, but most of my hitchhiking road mates were stoned out. When I got off the bus that afternoon in San Luis Obispo, I immediately connected with hippies like myself who were there in the city park, congregating, wondering what they were doing, and where they were going to go from there. They were from all over the nation; young people; wandering. I had been through that area a few times before, so I knew the direction I wanted to go. I wanted to head north on Route One along the coast towards Big Sur.

That part of the California coast is spectacular in natural scenic beauty. The water is breathtakingly blue, and the high craggy cliffs provide perfect vantage points for the shimmering ocean below. In the summer of 1965, and then again in the summer of 1966, I'd driven down the Big Sur Highway north to south, each time loving the experience, so I wanted to return and explore it some more. I put on my backpack, stuck out my thumb and hitchhiked my way through Morro Bay and Cambria. Later in the afternoon, I settled into a State Park campground on a cliff overlooking the Pacific Ocean in San Simeon Bay. I could see the famous Hearst Castle in the distance up on its mountain top. Night came, and the fog rolled in. I laid out my sleeping bag to get some needed sleep.

The next morning, I got up and went out to the road where I put out my thumb again, ready to start the cycle all over again. Right away, a large station wagon pulled over and a young guy with long shaggy hair and worn out clothes got out and told me to stash my backpack and climb aboard. I looked into the car stuffed with hippies who were passing joints around. There was no room for me, except if I crawled through its open back window into the rear of the storage area. I was able to squeeze in, leaving my backpack and sleeping bag dangling out the back. The station wagon then took off at high speed with this really strung out looking hippie guy behind the wheel.

The Big Sur highway is beautiful yet treacherous; a narrow, twisting and turning, roller coaster drive with one lane going in each direction. It hugs the Pacific Ocean for seventy-one miles along towering seaside cliffs with sheer drop-offs sometimes hundreds of feet below. It was a dangerous drive under normal conditions. I felt the car drifting and floating and I sensed that the weight in the back where I was riding was causing its front tires to lift off the road.

After about ten miles of this terror, I yelled out –

"Stop! Stop this car!"

The driver kept driving, so I yelled out again as loud as I could – "Stop this car, Man! Stop it right now!"

He finally pulled over and stopped and I quickly jumped out the back window with my pack and sleeping bag.

The hippies inside were going: "Oh wow, Man... What's with this dude... "

"What's wrong, Man? What's wrong with you, Man?"

They were all so stoned out of their minds that none of them had a clue they could all be killed travelling like that. We had just passed by a sign on the road that read, "Esalen Institute." This was a famous retreat center in Big Sur, that had become known as a center for the then emerging human potential and New Age movements. I needed an excuse to offer the hippies, so I told them I just wanted to visit Esalen.

Their response was, "Oh, wow Man... What a weird dude Man... Why would you want to go there?"

They then took off, leaving me on the side of the road where I thanked God I had gotten out of that car. Within no time, I got picked up again and continued on up the road, thinking that at any turn I might see the wreckage of the car with their bodies strewn about. It didn't happen.

After many days and nights of camping and hitchhiking up Big Sur highway, on the road with the hippies and other characters, I came into San Jose and bought another Greyhound bus ticket north. This was a twenty-hour-long ride to Portland, Oregon.

I arrived late at night to another dirty, downtown skid row Greyhound Bus station. Sleepy-eyed, I staggered off the bus and went to the luggage area where I stood in line to get my backpack. It wasn't there. The clerk at the window told me to hang tight until he could find out what happened to it. I had waited for about an hour when he told me that my bag had been located. Problem was, they had accidentally shipped it on to Spokane, Washington, way up north; but not to worry because if I was lucky, they might just ship it back on down to Portland sometime around two o'clock the next day. *Shit!* There I was, stuck in another drunken, derelict bus station late at night, with nothing but the coat on my back, a packet of cigarettes and the little I had in my wallet. I had no choice but to spend the night there; just wait it out until the next day to see if I could get my backpack back.

Sometimes life becomes too much to handle, so you just have to accept your situation and give in to it. In that creepy, dangerous, dark, bus terminal, I moved several times throughout the night from one filthy wooden bench to another, trying to avoid the spital and drizzle. Trying to avoid getting tangled up with the drunks, drug addicts, and criminals, who were seriously scoping out this young innocent-looking middle-class white kid they had in their midst. I was definitely a target, and I knew it, so I kept on the move, taking care of myself. I was there with the poor, the bums, the winos, the hobos, and the downtrodden of the earth. Like me, they had no other place to go, and though I feared them, I also felt a certain kinship with them. I was part of them and I think they picked up on my feelings, so they left me alone.

When I noticed the faintest rays of sun streaming through the bus terminal skylights that morning, I immediately went outside to greet the coming day. And what a day it was to be. I started walking through the waking city of Portland, thankful and happy to be escaping from the dangers and horrors of the bus depot. I set myself free and explored the entire downtown area on my own.

It was beautiful and refreshing to be out there on that morning in downtown Portland, Oregon on May 28, 1968. I bought donuts and hot chocolate at a stand in the early morning air and just sat back to enjoy them on a park bench in the center of town, when I noticed this young college kid nearby who was eagerly engaging workers passing by and handing out flyers. I walked over to him, took one of his flyers, then came back to my bench to finish my donuts and hot chocolate. He was a student campaigner working for the anti-war Presidential Democratic candidacy of Eugene McCarthy! How exciting! My sister Becky and I had walked door to door for McCarthy just the month before in Orange County. The flyer headlined the news that McCarthy was in Portland that day to ask Oregon Democrats for their votes. If he could capture the Oregon Democratic Party primary, and then California's primary, he could possibly become the national Democratic Party's nominee for President of the United States. The flyer also announced that he was scheduled to speak there later that day at 3:30 pm from a plaza platform in the heart of Portland's downtown office-and working-class district.

McCarthy's campaign was a true grassroots movement. At its core were thousands of young idealistic students, like this kid, traveling around the country with him, staying in run-down hotels from city to city, all fervently working against the war in Vietnam, working for and standing behind Eugene McCarthy— their torch bearer – to rescue our nation from its unbelievable nightmare. His campaign had been picking up lots of momentum in recent weeks, and it looked as if he might succeed. I introduced myself to this young activist, and we got to know each other. He invited me up to the McCarthy campaign headquarters which occupied several floors of a decrepit downtown Portland hotel; where hundreds of young students, were working away feverishly at desks, creating news releases, working at mimeograph machines (this was before copy machines), cranking out thousands of flyers, creating hand-lettered posters and banners. I was so thankful to be around such positive and hopeful energy.

It was such a frightening world for me to face then at barely twenty years of age. Everything was coming down on me: The Draft, the War; the prospect of getting across the border illegally into Canada. Even though I had travelled around the country a bit, I was still very unsure of myself. I had never been responsible for myself, mostly living at home where my mom and dad looked after and took care of me. They had cooked my meals and fed me, took care of the bills, housed me, and took care of all my needs until that time. So, there I was in downtown Portland, Oregon, without my backpack, trying to make sense of things and survive on my own.

I made it back to the Greyhound Bus Terminal at 2PM. Miraculously, they had recovered it! There was my backpack.

I picked it up, hugged and kissed it - then I walked back to watch Eugene McCarthy give his speech. This turned out to be a spellbinding and inspiring event that held me in awe as he extolled the crowd to demand that America should absolutely, immediately withdraw its military forces from Vietnam. It was an impressive speech, but I knew then that I had to get out of Portland. I had to regain some sense of myself, some sense of peace and solitude and security in my life. I really was getting weary at this point and I needed a place of seclusion, a place to think about things and collect my thoughts.

Two years before, in June 1966, the day after graduating from high school, my best friend Randy and I took off in his Volkswagen bug, on an epic six-week camping adventure around much of the western United States. We visited Yellowstone National Park, the Grand Teton's and Glacier National Park in Montana, before heading north into Canada. We toured the Canadian Rockies. Camping along the way, we headed west to British Columbia and Victoria Island, then drove south along the Pacific Coast Highway where we stayed for a few nights in the small beach town of Cannon Beach, Oregon. I really loved the place. After listening to McGovern's speech that afternoon, I returned to the Portland bus station and bought a 5 PM bus ticket straight out for Cannon Beach, which I had remembered. I found and rented a beachfront cottage on the sand where I could hear the wild howling of the wind and experience the near continuous driving rain and the dark thundering powerful crashing of the surf. There were no restaurants in this tiny town, but my cottage had a small stove and refrigerator, so I stopped by a local market and bought hot dogs and canned chili, canned soup and some crackers, tea and apples, cigarettes and some other things. I didn't know how to cook but I had brought along a can opener and could open a can and I also had a camping mess kit, so I made do.

On that part of the coast in Oregon it is almost always very stormy. I had no phone, no TV, no radio, no news. No connection with anything. I knew no one, and I was just there alone separated from everyone. I went out and walked for miles and miles in the rain during the days along those beautiful storm-driven beaches. I had the shore all to myself with all of its incredible power. During this time my mind was consumed with the war and what I was going to do with my life. I had started out my journey intending to escape to Canada but now I was not so sure. I had heard during my travels on the road that officials on both sides of the border were on the lookout for draft dodgers like me and that there was a high likelihood that the authorities would arrest me if I tried to cross over. I had lots of other doubts.

After a few days, I went into town and picked up a local newspaper. To my utter amazement and joy I read the headline that Eugene McCarthy had won the Oregon Democratic primary, defeating Robert Kennedy, his major opponent. It elated me that there just might be a chance that America was going to come to its senses and find a way out of the Vietnam War by electing him. McCarthy and his campaign then packed up and moved their operation down south to Los Angeles for the California Democratic primary election. I thought that if McCarthy could take the California Primary, then most likely he would get the national Democratic nomination as President and that would put an end to the Vietnam War. I was very excited about this possibility.

I had been on the road for about a month by then with no contact with anyone I knew. Homesick and weary I found a phone booth (there were no cell phones then) and called home.

Mom had been worrying about me since I left home and she was thrilled to get my call. We talked for quite a while before she told me the news. My Draft Notice had arrived in the mail, just as I thought it would, and it ordered me to report to the Los Angeles Induction Center in about three weeks. She asked me what I was going to do. She told me that she and my dad had talked seriously about my situation and they both strongly felt I would be better off to come back home, face it, and submit. We spoke for a while longer before I told her I had to go, but I would think about it. My mom was about the best mom a kid could ever have, and I always listened to and took her wise advice seriously. She was a highly intelligent and loving mother.

This was decision-making time. The harrowing adventures of the road had worn me out and I wanted off it. I humbly realized I wasn't the cavalier, carefree, vagabond type I had thought I was. "The long, strange trip" was too much for me to handle and was coming to its end. I spent the evening in the beachfront cottage wrestling with everything, thinking and imagining it all repeatedly. It came down to this: I had nothing to do with the Vietnam War and its creation or its propagation and I wanted nothing to do with it, yet they were placing me between a rock and a hard place, forcing me to make a pivotal decision. It was possible that if McCarthy could win the election, the war could end before I would end up being sent there.

I took the bus early the next morning to the Portland Airport and flew back down to LA, arriving home later in the evening.

It was just a few days later, in my parent's house, when my friend Gerry woke me in my bedroom. While I was rubbing the sleep out of my eyes, Gerry said,

"Well, what do you think about the news last night?".

"What news? I went to bed early last night, and I didn't watch the news."

"You didn't hear? They assassinated Robert Kennedy last night!"

Robert Kennedy had defeated Eugene McCarthy in the California Primary election the night before, after which he immediately declared his victory. I watched it on TV, then turned it off and went to bed.

I was asleep when the assassin shot and killed him. It was another one of those devastating shocks that tore apart the soul of the nation during those years. When I heard the news, I accepted it as further validation of the feelings I'd been having for quite some time. There was something working here, way too powerful to deal with. The political world was broken. I accepted there were other powerful forces at play here, and that open resistance to it would be futile. After the assassination of Robert Kennedy, Eugene McCarthy's peace campaign dissolved in fear. This destroyed any remaining hope for the peace and anti-war movement within the Democratic Party. So much for politics. That was the end of that.

CHAPTER NINE

Basic Training

"WELCOME TO THE UNITED STATES ARMY AT FORT ORD! NOW, YOU PIECE-OF-STINKING-SHIT MAGGOTS GET YOUR SORRY ASSES OFF THIS BUS! AND DO THIS RIGHT NOW IF YOU KNOW WHAT'S GOOD FOR YOU, BECAUSE WE OWN YOUR SHIT NOW! MOVE, MOVE, MOVE!!!"

That was our welcoming message as we flew off the bus in sheer terror and did exactly whatever they ordered us to do. I had arrived with about fifty other conscripts on a bus from the Los Angeles Induction Center. It was ten at night, June 18, 1968, my enlistment date.

The United States Army's basic training camp at Fort Ord, California, was on the central California coast on the Monterey Bay, just north of the city of Monterey. It was a major US Army training facility; the place I first realized they had me. I was now owned by the US Army. They owned my skin and everything within and under it. Right away they threatened us with clubs and all, ordering us off the bus and onto the ground in rigid push-up position without resistance. They cussed us, demeaned us, and threatened to stomp us with their combat boots. They demanded we declare our allegiance to the cause of defeating the communists in Vietnam. We were all prisoners of theirs, to be processed like meat through their barbaric grinding war machine, and they wanted us to know this. Almost all of us were draftees who had been against the draft to begin with, and we resented being there. After getting off the bus and being kicked around, we were marched into a large, fluorescent-lit Quonset hut office building where Army clerks ordered us to take our seats at desks in the room. There they noted our arrival and took down our personal information, cross-checking it with our Selective Service files. We were the new material, the new raw meat, freshly arrived for their war.

There were some guys with us who were just not capable of withstanding the insanity of it all. "Smiley" was one of them. I first noticed him in the LA induction Center where he refused to answer when they called out his name. He'd been drafted and put on the same bus with the rest of us inductees and arrived when we arrived later that night at Fort Ord. I observed him along the way and noticed he was a strange guy. Though close to us in age, Smiley stood out as an old-style white greaser out of the fifties, like the late actor James Dean, with a long, greasy pompadour, hefty sideburns, upturned collar and all the rest. He was a throwback, different from the rest of us. He smoked one cigarette after another and said absolutely nothing along the way. Not a peep.

They called out our names in alphabetical order for us to respond "present." When they called Smiley's name, he did not respond. This stopped the process. They called out his name, Robert B. Smiley, again. No response. This went on and on, repeatedly, until someone finally tipped off the sergeant in charge who Smiley was. The staff sergeants took note, winked at each other and nodded as if to say, *okay, we understand, we've got another one of these fuckers.* They recorded Smiley as present anyway.

After hours and hours of paperwork shit, they marched us into a dim barracks to get some sleep. Though I was sure no one else wanted anything at all to do with him, I took the bunk right above Smiley's bunk. I felt sorry for him. He was a different dude and so was I, so I felt a certain bond with him because he was a rebel like me. I never spoke with him or heard a word come out of him.

The next morning, they marched us over to get our first Army haircuts. The barbers at the barbershop were all women, minimum wage civilian contract employees, instructed by the Army to shear our heads bald as if we were sheep. There was some legality in place that required them to ask each one of us recruits how we wanted our hair to be cut. It required them to ask this. Our Drill Instructors informed us of this ridiculous legality and ordered us to instruct the barbers to shear our heads bald, Army style. Those were our orders.

I was sitting in a row of chairs in the barbershop where we were being moved along from one chair to the next as our time to be sheared approached. Smiley with his greasy pompadour hair-do was sitting immediately to my left and was next up. When the barber motioned him up to her chair, he did so. She wrapped a towel around his neck, then as required by law, asked him how he wanted his hair to be cut. Smiley hesitated and didn't answer her. She repeated, "How do you want me to cut your hair?" It was then that I heard the first words come from Smiley's mouth since I had noticed him a few days earlier.

He simply said, "Give me a trim."

Upon hearing this, the woman picked up her shears, starting at the nape of his neck. Working straight up with her razor, she buzzed off a huge chunk of his hair. One half of his greasy pompadour came flopping down to the floor of the barbershop in one plump. When Smiley saw this, he became enraged, stood up in the chair with his eyes on fire, and loudly, angrily, yelled at the woman,

"You call yourself a barber!"

This scared the shit out of the woman, who screamed for help as he tore the towel off his neck and stumbled out the door of the barbershop. A crew of Drill Instructors immediately met him at the bottom of the doorstep, jumped him, and beat him severely into unconsciousness. They didn't stop. After they beat him unconscious, they seemed to take great perverse pleasure in twisting his arms and legs. They brought us all out to witness the barbarity, where I was sure I heard his joints popping. I watched the entire scene go down. We all did. After a while, things settled down and we returned to the barbershop. I took my place in line where I got my shearing. Later that day, we were given a lecture by the Drill Instructor in charge who warned us that if any of us should behave like Smiley, we would surely suffer a fate similar to his. He told us that Smiley, if he was to survive, would be sent to the Army's Fort Leavenworth Prison where he would spend the rest of his life breaking rocks and doing hard time. It was all a lesson for us to learn from and consider.

Officially, our basic training program had not even begun. This was because there were so many draftees arriving for Vietnam that they had no place to put us. For the next two weeks, before the official beginning date of our training cycle, they marched us every morning uphill, within the base where these old two-story, weather beaten, wooden World War II-era Army barracks stood, row after row, street after street. These old boarded up barracks, painted in faded shades of Army green, had probably not been used since the Korean War, fifteen years earlier. They ordered us to remove the old plywood from the buildings doors and windows and clean them up for our own use before we would move into them two weeks later. Each two-story barracks housed forty soldiers— one platoon. Fort Ord, along the Monterey Bay Pacific coast, was a dreary, foggy place, always cold and damp. They ordered us to keep the windows open at night to prevent the spread of spinal meningitis, which had been killing soldiers on the base.

Our basic training company was comprised of one hundred and sixty trainees organized into four platoons of forty men each. Each platoon had a Drill Instructor Sergeant in charge. Each of these platoon Sergeants reported to a Master Sergeant Drill Instructor, who then reported to a Company First Sergeant. The Company First Sergeant then reported to the Company Commander, a Captain, an officer in charge of the company. Our basic training company was one of four companies that made up a Battalion. There were several battalions training there during that summer of 1968 at Fort Ord, comprising tens of thousands of us young draftees.

Our Drill Instructors were mostly uneducated, young bullies, who had been taken in by the Army and all its nonsense propaganda. When I arrived at Fort Ord in June 1968, many of the drill instructors were soldiers fresh back from combat tours in Vietnam and they seemed pretty crazy to us. The condition known as PTSD (Post Traumatic Stress Disorder) had yet to be diagnosed and classified by the mental health profession, but it was easy to see that something was wrong with these guys. They were brutal to us at times and even seemed to take sadistic pleasure as they abused us. Neither they nor the Army were aware of their sick conditions, yet these sick characters were put in charge of us, set free like beasts upon prey.

The Army's Basic Training Program conditioned us for the horrors of war, both physically and mentally. Their goal was to strip us of who and what we thought we were as civilian individuals before we entered the military, to recondition our bodies and remold our minds into becoming non-thinking military robots, able to respond as a group at their command. Brain-washing was an essential ingredient of the training. We were not to think of ourselves as individuals.

After being at Fort Ord for two weeks, getting our barracks ready, our basic training program officially began. Every morning, our company of 160 men would go out on long, punishing runs; led by, pushed and prodded by our Drill Instructors screaming endless threats. We ran in strict company formation, four abreast, wearing our new blister-causing combat boots. We ran for miles and miles. At first, we got sick and puked our guts out on the sides of the road as they forced us to continue running. You had to keep running because if you didn't and you fell behind, the platoon coming up behind was encouraged to stomp upon you. The Drill Instructors gleefully laughed with each other and took great pleasure in this madness. Combat boots of the soldiers coming up behind you just might get your skull crushed if you fell behind and couldn't continue running.

Much of their efforts involved trying to turn us trainees against each other. They made all suffer because of the mistakes or inability of one or a few. If, after a run, a soldier just couldn't keep up with the rest of the company, they would hold us all accountable and stand us at rigid attention. They would then identify the trainee who was the cause for our suffering. The penalty was often something like ordering all of us, the entire company of 160 men, onto the ground in rigid push-up position for lengthy periods of time on the hot asphalt. This, after a day of exhausting physical and mental humiliation. They encouraged us to get even in off-hours with those trainees responsible for our suffering. They encouraged what they called "Blanket Parties" or "GI Showers." In the middle of the night, in a darkened barracks, cowardly, anonymous trainees from other barracks would find out where the poor kid who'd screwed up was, find his bunk where he slept, cover him with a blanket and beat the shit out of him.G.I.Showers were similar. They would take a young guy into a barracks shower room and scrub him bloody with a hard bristle scrub brush. The trainees who were attacked in this way were usually the younger, immature kids who were struggling just to keep up in basic training. They didn't know what was happening to them. They were left there, beaten up and crying in the shower, unable to understand. It was these who were so often viciously attacked.

I vividly recall a conversation I overheard between our Company Commander West Point appointed, an Army Captain in charge of our company, and my platoon Drill Sergeant, regarding one of our company's young, immature, childlike, trainees who couldn't get with the program. The Captain told the Sergeant if the kid couldn't do what they expected of him and get with the program, it didn't matter because he would eventually just be sent on to Vietnam to be wasted anyway. The message was not to feel sorry for him. We all just had to do our job; turn our heads and look the other way. There was no allowance for mercy.

While running, we were continuously ordered to sing out the war chants the Drill Instructors had memorized by heart in their Drill Instructor's schools. They usually went something like this:

"I want-a-be an Airborne Ranger
I want to live a life of danger
I Want-a Go to Viet-Nam
I Want-a Kill a Viet-Cong
With a Knife or With A Gun
Either Way, it Will Be Good Fun
Stomp 'Em, Beat 'Em, Kick 'Em In The Ass
Hide Their Bodies In The Grass
I want-a go to Vietnam. Just to kill Ol' Charlie Cong
Am I right or wrong? Am I goin' strong?
Am I right or wrong?"

They drilled chants like these into us continuously throughout basic training, as we marched and ran, and these chants almost always involved how much we wanted to kill. They required us to chant them. If a drill instructor thought you were not yelling out and shouting their chants at the tops of your lungs, you might then be taken aside and threatened or punished. You had to make them think they were in complete control of not just your body but of your mind as well. The whole thing was one continuous physical and mental hell. They marched us and ran us every day into exhaustion from before dawn till late after dusk. We hardly got any sleep, and we were sick most of the time.

Sometimes they would order us into air-conditioned auditoriums and force us to sit in chairs at attention and watch professionally produced war propaganda films. The films were about the supposed horrible crimes of the Communist Viet-Cong, and how it was essential that we American soldiers, in the name of freedom and liberty, go to Vietnam to save the people of Vietnam from the evil communist monsters. We needed to go to Vietnam to kill them. The Drill Instructors monitored you to see if you were paying attention or not. If they suspected you might doze off or not pay attention to the propaganda, you would definitely be singled out and punished.

"What is 'The Spirit of the Bayonet' men?"

"It is To Kill, Drill Sergeant! To Kill Without Mercy, Drill Sergeant!"

They would march us to a sandy lot and issue us an eleven-pound M14 Combat Rifle stock with a twelve-inch bayonet mounted on its muzzle. Bayonet training was an enormous deal that took up much of our time and energy. They wanted us to become used to the idea of killing with it. We would spend hours and hours every day practicing, drilling, stabbing tires that hung from chains and other obstacles that represented the enemy. They taught us the fine arts of the use of the rifle and the bayonet. You could kill the enemy by crushing his skull with the butt of your rifle or just by parrying and stabbing him in the eye or anywhere else. There were so many ways to kill a man with the rifle and the fixed bayonet.

Other days we were marched out into the interior of the massive scrub brushland areas that comprised Fort Ord, where we were subjected to other classes. There was a class on how to throw grenades. They taught us how to hold the grenade and pull the plug, then release the trigger, and count to three before you threw it into the "sump," and it exploded and killed you and everyone around you.

On another day came the tear-gas class. They took us all out to a compound in the hills where there was a bare, windowless, cinderblock building. They took twenty of us at a time into the building. Once inside, the Army Chemical Warfare Staff on hand, all wearing gas masks, shut the door, and ordered us to form a circle around a table that had been set up in the center of the room. None of us trainees were allowed to wear our gas masks. They ordered us to grab the shoulder of the soldier standing to our immediate right and informed us they were going to set off a tear gas cannister in the closed-up room. We were then told the door would remain locked during the entire exercise that required us to achieve a specific goal, as a group, before they would unlock the door and release us from the gas chamber. The order was that all twenty of us in that gas chamber, without gas masks, were to march continuously around in an unbroken circle, completing ten rotations before they would open the doors for us to escape. If anyone broke the chain, the group would remain in the gas chamber until we accomplished the required rotations. My group accomplished it, but we were all vomiting and exploding shit out of our sinuses and asses for days after.

One of the most memorable experiences in basic training was a class given to us by Army Special Forces Green Berets. These instructors were expertly trained in the very specific art of how to easily kill a man, in near-intimate ways. The object of this class was to impart to us as much of their knowledge as they could in a single day, and they spared none of the gory details. It was so easy to understand, so easily done, and there was nothing emotional about it. It was almost always a simple thing to do. The usual weapons, like guns and knives, weren't even necessary. Many everyday objects could do the job: a broken bottle, or a shard of broken pottery, a strand of wire, a gardening tool, a hammer, even a pencil or ballpoint pen. The list was endless, as were the methods. The key element to consider when killing a man, if the victim was not detained and under control, was almost always the element of surprise. Once this was attained you could just use your imagination and let it go wild with how you were going to rip out a throat or cut a jugular, pulverize a skull, or destroy an eye. We realized these guys had lots of experience with this subject which they so thoroughly enjoyed teaching.

While most of the guys who went through the insanity of basic training could maintain a certain level of mental balance, there were a few guys who couldn't handle it. One guy in my platoon wanted out in any way possible. He tried to get out of it the same way my friend Steve had tried, by becoming physically disabled. The guy paid another trainee, a huge powerful kid in our platoon, to lift him up high over his head and throw him on his back directly onto the ground with all his might. He hoped that his back or neck might break so he would be taken away and given a medical discharge. An ambulance did come and take him away, but we never heard what happened to him. There were lots of stories like this going around; stories about guys standing up in the line of fire at the rifle ranges or on the machine gun fire ranges, demanding that they be shot and killed right there on the spot. Anything to get out of going to Vietnam. I could go on and on describing the horrors I experienced during those ten weeks while there at Fort Ord, California, in the summer of 1968.

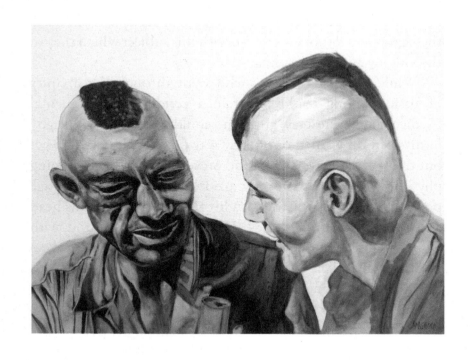

Drill Instructor with Lieutenant

When I arrived at Fort Ord in June 1968, many of our drill instructors were soldiers fresh back from tours in Vietnam and I'm sure they were unaware of their Post-Traumatic Stress Disorder (PTSD); a diagnosis that was unknown then that disabled so many. Neither they nor the Army were aware of their sick conditions. Yet it was these sick characters who the Army put in charge of us young, drafted recruits, set free like beasts upon prey.

CHAPTER TEN

Not Paid Eleven Cents an Hour to Think

TOWARD THE END of our basic training cycle, our company went out into the boonies camping for a few days and nights in something that the Army called a "Bivouac." It was supposed to be a simulated combat-like experience. They took us out, marching around within the vast expanse and confines of the backwoods of Fort Ord until we arrived at our prearranged camp site. This was way up in the hills amongst the trees and bushes. We arrived at around noon. It was lunchtime, and we were all starving. Immediately, each platoon, and each squad, was ordered to set up two-man pup tents, then dig a large foxhole in front of it. We set to work doing this quickly and when we were finished, the word was out that a mess tent (field kitchen) was up and running and serving hot meals for us. When I heard this, I picked up my mess kit and headed straight for the tent. I traveled the pathways to the mess tent, found my place in line, got served, then headed back to my tent and foxhole to enjoy my lunch. When I returned to my foxhole with my food, my buddies informed me I was in terrible trouble. Terrible trouble!

Soon after I had left the foxhole to get my lunch, an inspection entourage had arrived to look around. This entourage was headed up by none other than the Basic Training Base Commander, Colonel Edmonds. When they came around to my foxhole, the Colonel noticed there was a rifle laying unattended. That was my rifle. In the Army they drill you repeatedly to have great respect for your rifle. While they check it out to you, you must never leave it unattended. It's a cardinal sin. Doing so could be a Court Marshal offense. When the Colonel saw this, he picked up my rifle and asked who it belonged to. My buddies finked on me and told him: it was Private Gibson's rifle. The Company Commander then told my buddies to tell me I was ordered to report immediately to the Officer's Mess Tent to retrieve it.

After gobbling down my lunch, I approached the Officer's Mess Tent prepared for the worst and presented myself at attention to the Sergeant who was on duty. He loudly announced my name. I glanced inside the large canvas tent to observe what was going on in there. They'd set up a long table where twenty or thirty officers and Drill Sergeants were eating chow together while Colonel Edmonds, like a god, presided at the head of the table. To his right and to his left sat all of his suck-up, junior officers and NCOs. When my name was called out, I realized they could see and hear me standing there. They'd been expecting me and were thrilled to see I had arrived and presented myself for their lunchtime entertainment. When my name was announced, one of our Company Drill Sergeants rose from the table and came over. He stood just a few inches away from my face and screamed and yelled and threatened me for my offense of leaving my rifle unattended.

"Private Gibson! Do you realize the seriousness of your dereliction of duty here by leaving your unattended rifle in your foxhole?"

Standing there as rigid as I could, I yelled back to him even more loudly, "YES, DRILL SERGEANT!!!"

He went on and on like this and I kept repeating back to him at the top of my lungs,

"YES, DRILL SERGEANT, YES DRILL SERGEANT..."

I stood at rigid attention at the entrance to the mess tent receiving his abuse, then noticed a young recently graduated West Point junior Lieutenant who had just transferred into our company, who tapped the sergeant administering my abuse on the shoulder and ordered him to sit down. The Lieutenant was going to take over the show. He had something on his mind he was hoping would impress the officers and others there, especially the Colonel. He was going to use some kind of psychological approach, some kind of game. They were all sitting there munching on their lunchtime chow, enjoying the show when the young West Pointer asked me,

"Private Gibson, you know obviously that you have committed a very serious violation of one of the United States Army's rules and regulations, do you not?!"

I screamed back at him, "YES SIR!!!"

"Private Gibson, you know that you have committed this offense, am I right!"

"YES SIR, I AM AWARE OF THIS SIR! YOU ARE RIGHT SIR!"

Then he said, "Well Private Gibson, if you are aware of and admit to this offense then I am going to ask you a very simple question." After he said this, the men in the mess tent perked up and observed more intently, wondering what this incompetent little asshole West Pointer Lieutenant had up his sleeve. They were primarily career Army lifers and had disdain for this kind of cadet rooky who knew nothing at all about Army life yet carried on with an air of superiority.

The Lieutenant then loudly put his mysterious question to me as if it were like an interrogation or something. "Private Gibson, you are standing here freely admitting your guilt so I want you to tell me now, what your punishment should be!"

I screamed back at him, "PRIVATE GIBSON DOES NOT KNOW, SIR!!!"

Upon my response, he shouted the same question to me, I screamed back at him again, "PRIVATE GIBSON DOES NOT KNOW SIR!!!"

At this point he was getting physically agitated and screamed repeatedly his question about what I thought my punishment should be. I kept repeating back to him as loudly as I could,

"SIR, PRIVATE GIBSON DOES NOT KNOW, SIR!!!"

He was really getting frustrated and pissed-off, and I felt I could be in for a lot of shit soon if I didn't give him some kind of an answer right away. It was then that the perfect answer came to me.

From day one in Basic Training, they drilled into our heads continuously that we were stupid nothings and that our thoughts did not amount to a thing. They considered us to be nothing other than tools to obey their commands without question. We were not to think on our own. One of their favorite lines to scream at us was, "You are not paid

Eleven Cents an hour to think!" (this was literally accurate as we were actually on duty twenty-four hours a day, seven days a week, and our monthly salary was something like seventy-nine dollars.)

Standing at rigid attention, I screamed back at him the most basic thing that we had been taught while there at basic training all those weeks....

"SIR, PRIVATE GIBSON DOES NOT KNOW, BECAUSE PRIVATE GIBSON IS NOT PAID ELEVEN CENTS AN HOUR TO THINK, SIR!!!"

This brought the house down. I swear I saw Colonel Edmonds spit his food out in hysterical laughter when I said this. All the others in there were also laughing like hell as the West Pointer stood in embarrassment like a dumb shit, not knowing what to do. He ordered me to the ground to do a hundred push-ups as punishment, then to take my rifle back to my foxhole and never let this happen again.

I said, "Yes, Sir."

CHAPTER ELEVEN

New Orders

BASIC TRAINING WAS finally ending, and I had somehow squeaked through. Just a few days before our graduation ceremony was to take place, I was informed that my new orders had arrived. I was to report for further advanced military training to Fort Sam Houston, Texas, to be trained as an Army Combat Medical Corpsman. I had it in mind when I got drafted that if I was going to have to submit to the draft, I would do everything in my power to become an Army Medic. That was because I was opposed to the Vietnam War and to the idea of being sent there as an infantry soldier, with orders to kill Vietnamese people with whom I had no argument. That was something I couldn't live with. I thought that if I had to go to Vietnam, then I would go there to *save* lives, not take lives.

They selected me to become an Army Medic because of decisions I consciously made upon arriving at Fort Ord at the beginning of Basic Training. When I first arrived at Fort Ord, they set all of us down in rooms at tables for batteries of examinations and testing that went on for hours. They tested our IQs, our strengths, weaknesses, and everything else. They wanted to know who we were and what we were made of, both physically and mentally; this in order for them to know where to place us most effectively within their ranks, according to our profiles. I easily figured out how to answer their questions to fit within the profile of a soldier who would most likely fit the template of an Army medic. It was easy to figure out. They didn't want guys to train as medics who would be better suited to become snipers, infantry grunts, truck drivers, mechanics, cooks, or anything else. When presented with simple, multiple-choice questions like: "What would you most likely prefer? Going camping and hunting with my buddies or going to the library and reading poetry?", I of course chose the intellectual option of going to the library. At the end of their questioning, they also asked us what we would like to do while in the Army, what Military Occupational Service (MOS), we would like to be assigned to. I answered, "Army Medical Corpsman."

Another important thing I pulled off in Basic Training was to become the lowest scoring rifleman in our entire Basic Training Company. This was part of my plan. That's right, I became the worst shot of all one-hundred and sixty of us. I intentionally missed the targets and scored at the bottom, even though I had been raised by my dad shooting guns and was a good shot. Every Army basic trainee had to pass a minimal score at the rifle range, or else they would send him back for another round of basic training, a horrible prospect. I barely passed my final rifle range test, so I was obviously not going to be a candidate for something like sniper's school.

There was also one other powerful reason the Army chose me to become a medic, and it had nothing to do with me personally. America was sustaining massive casualties in Vietnam at the time, and the Army sorely needed medics.

Our families were invited to come and watch us graduate

from basic training. Mom and Dad and my sister Becky, who was nearly four months pregnant, made the long trip up from Orange County for the occasion. I had been a virtual prisoner at Fort Ord, locked within its gates for twelve weeks, and it meant everything in the world to me that they did this. I was given an off-base pass for a few hours after the ceremony, and we drove into the town of Monterrey where they were staying. We went to a nice restaurant, had dinner together, then drove to the hotel and talked with each other for a few hours until it was time for me to report back to the base. I'm sure Mom and Dad were surprised and relieved to see I had somehow managed to *just* get through basic training. I knew they'd had their doubts. But Becky was concerned about me for another reason. We'd been close siblings and I knew she was concerned about my state of mind. She was observing my mental condition, wondering if I was okay or if they'd taken me.

Early the next morning I left the cold, damp, environment of Fort Ord, wearing a newly issued warm woolen Army Dress Green uniform. I boarded an older turboprop Army Troop Transport plane with other soldiers and flew six hours from Fort Ord all the way to San Antonio, Texas. It was a boiling and tropically humid day in late August 1968 when I arrived. The heat nearly suffocated me, in my woolen uniform, when they jammed us all under a canvas-covered troop truck on top of our duffle bags to transport us from the airport to the

base.

CHAPTER TWELVE

Army Combat Medics School

FORT SAM HOUSTON lies in the heart of historic San Antonio, Texas, near the Alamo. It's the headquarters of the United States Army's Medical Command Center, an emotionally heavy place with a deeply sad military history—the history of those who deal with consequences of the carnage of war. This was where I was sent to be trained as an Army Combat Medic. My particular training company headquarters office displayed on its walls the many awards for bravery and sacrifice given out to its graduates throughout its history, spanning several wars. There were several Medals of Honor, earned by and awarded to its graduates. Many other high-level medals were there as well. There were literally hundreds of citations. What was so sad to me was that many of those ribbons and medals had been awarded posthumously. Medics throughout American history have a very proud and legendary history of giving their all and dying for their country.

Army Combat Medics School was the most grueling education one can imagine. Within a few days of my arrival, our classes started. Right away they started showing us films depicting in graphic detail the kinds of catastrophic wounds and injuries we medics would be expected to deal with once in Vietnam; blown away faces and half-blown away skulls; sucking chest wounds, traumatic amputations, and all the rest. Blood and guts were everywhere. Several guys got sick to their stomachs and threw up or passed out onto the classroom floors as they forced us to watch these movies. They gave us live courses on how to start IVs, how to perform an emergency tracheostomy, and how to insert and maintain an airway, how to perform CPR, apply a tourniquet, or inject morphine. The course covered everything one could think of. Our training was intensive and excellent.

During this time, I received a few very illegal but gratefully appreciated care packages from back home during mail call. These were sent by my old loyal friend Randy. He sent several carefully wrapped marijuana joints and a few rolls of the pep pills known as Bennies. These made me very popular amongst the guys in our training company as I would sometimes invite my closest buddies to join me down by the creek to share with them and get high with me in the very early morning, just to take the edge off before we would start our training for the day.

Medic's school was an intense ten weeks of training where we were taught to save and care for our fellow soldiers' sometimes catastrophic combat wounds. They drilled it into us that our soldiers would depend on us for their very survival. I took my training seriously and did my best to study and learn as much as I could. At the end of our course, I finished close to the top of my class, ninth out of nearly two-hundred and fifty trained Corpsmen.

I remember the day I received my orders for Vietnam. Our

final classes were over for the day when our sergeants ordered us out of the barracks to stand at attention. Something very important was about to happen. When the Company was all present and accounted for, they announced what this was all about. Our Orders had arrived. They then marched from man to man passing out envelopes to each soldier. These were our orders commanding us to our next Army duty assignments. After we received our envelopes, we were ordered to fall out of formation, and we were excused for the day. Nearly every one of us received orders for Vietnam. This was when the shit really hit the fan! After the company opened their envelopes and read that most of them had been ordered to Vietnam they pretty much went nuts and rioted; tipping over bunks and wall lockers, destroying just about everything inside the barracks, while screaming things like "Fuck the Army !!!" and "Hell No! I won't Go!" They then brought out their stashed-away booze, exasperating the situation. Soon the base MPs were called in with drawn pistols to restore order.

After I got the news, I quietly left the company area and walked by myself through the streets to the local base Post Exchange to get a beer. Nothing seemed to matter anymore. My mind was stunned upon the realization that the very thing I had been running from had happened. They'd gotten from me exactly what they had wanted all along. Even though I knew these orders were probably coming, I was stunned.

CHAPTER THIRTEEN

Home on Leave

I HAD BEEN away from home for more than five months during my military training. The plane departing San Antonio took off that evening with only a few passengers onboard and I plugged in my headphones, kicked back and listened to Glen Campbell crooning his tune "Wichita Lineman." I had been completely locked away and separated from the world I had known. Becky and Bob picked me up at the LA Airport that night. They wanted to know all about what I'd been through. They were curious about how my experiences had changed me.

Becky told me all about the violent political anti-war protests and police riots that had broken out in Chicago in late August of that year. I had been unaware. She told me all about the Democratic Party's Presidential Nominating Convention of 1968 which destroyed the Democratic Party as a peace party when they nominated the Vietnam War enabler, Hubert Humphrey, as their candidate. Politics, as a solution to stop the war, was over.

I came home to the loving arms of my parents that night after more than five months of hell. When I awoke the next morning, there was a terrible ringing in my ears, a nonstop sound that wouldn't go away. I had no idea what was causing it. My mother and father were kind to me during this time. I wanted to go out to see what had been happening in the world since I'd been gone. Dad loaned me his car. Donning my new military haircut, I revisited the old quad for a few days at the Fullerton Junior College Campus. The quad had been where we'd sit around talking not only about what beer-bust parties were happening that week, but also about what we were learning in our philosophy, anthropology, science, and history classes. A major topic of discussion had been the Vietnam War and how we felt about it. I went back there just to catch up on things I'd missed since I'd been gone.

I engaged in a conversation with a guy, an Anaheim High grad, who was sitting there on the wall in the quad where we used to sit. He was a student, a few years older than I, who'd recently returned from a combat tour in Vietnam and was now out of the Army and free, attending college on the G.I. Bill. He was very anti-war and very thankful he had survived his tour. When I told him about my situation, he listened to my story with careful attention. I told him that even though I was opposed to the war and didn't want to go, I felt I had to go to take care of the wounded. He looked at me and told me with all sincerity that he had great respect for me and my decision.

While I was home, I contacted some of my old friends to tell them I was back. They invited me to a few parties, but I found that my new military appearance was not very hip. I was a turnoff to them and not well-accepted. People shied away from me and I picked up on it. Just five months before, with my long hair and hippie garb, I was in with the in-crowd, well thought of and popular. But now that I had the military look, and was obviously headed for Vietnam, they wanted little to do with me. I wasn't cool anymore, and they kept their psychological distance. They rejected me, and I could definitely feel it. Phonies.

At one party, I sat down for a conversation over beers to talk with another guy who was just a few years older than myself. He told me he had an exemption from military service; he had a good job, was married, and living happily with his wife and two young children. He had no worries at all. I left the party that night with the sad realization that I was on my way to a war I did not believe in, where I might get killed, without ever having the chance to have a life with kids of my own. I felt cheated.

Those three weeks of leave were a depressing time for me. The night before I was to leave for Vietnam I went to a Thanksgiving dinner held at my older brother JC's house, attended by my mother and father and the rest of the family. JC and my father were adamant war hawks who strongly believed that what our country was doing in Vietnam was the moral good and right thing for our country to do. They knew how I felt. The conversation around the table that evening was subdued as we all realized that the very next morning, I was going to report for duty to a war that they strongly believed in, a war I did not believe in, yet I would be the one required to lay my life on the line for *their* beliefs.

Here I was home again, after over twenty weeks of unbelievable hell, facing a huge decision. Would I report and go to the war the next morning or would I run and hide? Everything was spinning wildly in my mind. As the hour drew near, I gave in and followed the flow. I realized I might die in Vietnam and I was alone with my decision. I made my choice. During my leave, I spent hours alone, contemplating all that life had taught me until then. Once again, I analyzed my political, spiritual, and religious experiences; my meditation; my travels, and most recently, my military experiences. My thoughts then came together as a revelation. Once again, the realization came to me that my life was an illusory thing. I was existing in a temporal, dualistic world; an ever-changing world of the "Ten thousand things." This truth had been spoken and written of in countless languages and understood by humanity throughout millennia in countless ways. I just had to learn to "flow with it," to accept and live a life in the awareness of ever-changing reality–live in the awareness that life will continue to go on. This spiritual truth was so beautifully expressed in the lyrics of a popular Beatles song –

Life flows on within you and without you

Again, I restate the comment I made at the beginning of this narrative,

We come into this world, not knowing from one moment to the next what is going to happen to us. Did we ask for this? I don't think so, and I don't believe in God or pre-ordination. Things just happen to us, and we try to make the best of whatever we are presented with. I think this is the basic truth of our existence– we just try to make the best of things as they come to us.

CHAPTER FOURTEEN

Headed for Vietnam

IT WAS LATE November 1968 when Mom and Dad drove me to the bus station. Both had tears in their eyes. We hugged and said our goodbyes as I boarded the bus to leave. Dad was trying to hide his emotions but was crying and trembling as he called out to me, "Give 'em hell, Jim!" They were sad and frightened. I tried to hide my tears too as I boarded the bus. We knew there was a fairly good chance I would never see them again. I instinctively knew that if I could survive the war and make it home alive, I would probably never be the same. I rode the morning bus into LAX, where I caught an early civilian flight to Oakland Airport. A military bus took me and some other soldiers from there to the Oakland Army Terminal. This was a sprawling World War II-era Army complex of buildings and warehouses on the docks in Oakland, on the San Francisco Bay. It was a major facility that the US Army used to gather and ship men to Vietnam. Large and sometimes very violent demonstrations against the war had been held there, organized by anti-war student radicals from the nearby Berkeley University.

The Oakland Terminal was a scary, seedy, intimidating

place: cold, stark, and dark. It was dirty, and it stunk. I spent the next two days and nights gathered in that place where thousands of young guys like myself were being readied, just waiting in those vast warehouses, to be shipped over to Vietnam. We stood in long lines for hours and were issued our new combat jungle fatigues and boots. We were being prepared for what to expect upon arrival in Vietnam.

There were multi-level bunk beds where we were supposed to rest in these dark, cave-like warehouse rooms. We were strangers to each other. Thousands had passed through this place before us – like cattle waiting for the slaughterhouse. We each waited for our names and serial numbers to be called. Eventually my number was called, and I boarded a transport bus to Travis Air Force Base just north of Oakland. We took off just before sunrise and flew to Honolulu, landing on a dazzlingly bright December morning. We got off the plane and waited around for a few hours for refueling and supplies. The flight also took on more passengers - soldiers, mostly.

It had been cold and stormy when we flew out of Travis Air Force Base that morning, but it was sunny and beautiful in Honolulu. During the time on the ground, I stared out the terminal windows at the colorful Hawaiian Mountains in the distance and had serious thoughts of running - *deserting* - escaping the airfield, escaping Vietnam and running away into those mountains.

After a few hours we got back on the plane, took off, and headed west across the great blue Pacific. I remember looking out the window and seeing how the tiny ships and islands looked from eight miles high. I noticed the female flight attendants seemed less attractive than the ones on the flight from California to Honolulu.

After a few hours, we descended again. The word was out

that we were to land at Wake Island. There had been a WWII propaganda film produced starring John Wayne that had made this tiny island famous. The movie was about the historic battle that took place there, early during the Japanese-American Pacific War in the early forties, when the Japanese attacked and took the island from our military forces. It was a bloody mess. All the marines died valiantly trying to hold the island. We were coming in for our landing, and as the plane got down to near water level, I realized I couldn't see a runway beneath us, only water. Just as the plane touched down, the plane's wheels found the runway as the pilot put the aircraft into a major effort to stop. We refueled, dropped off and took on more passengers, then took off again.

We flew a few thousand miles further southwest to Okinawa, Japan, and the US Air base which would prepare us for our last leg of the journey into Vietnam. Okinawa is another island famous in American military lore for the WWII battle that cost the lives of thousands of American soldiers. We landed, deplaned and marched to an airport terminal where they ordered us to stand by until our flight was ready. It was warmer there in Okinawa—hot, humid air. The number of military aircraft landing and taking off from this base was phenomenal.

While standing around and waiting in the terminal, a large jet transport landed, and a group of soldiers deplaned then began walking towards us. They were just coming back from their tours in Vietnam. So many of the men looked tired and beaten down, their ragged uniforms a mess. They were a disturbing sight. Their eyes were dark. There were no smiles. And they mostly looked down as they walked past and away from us. They made brief eye contact; like they didn't want to see us, nor us to see them. They didn't want to say anything to us or have anything to do with us. The contrast of mood and character between those of us who were on our way to Vietnam, and those who were coming out of Vietnam could not have been more frighteningly apparent. The mood of our flight became noticeably anxious at the sight of these men. Guys were asking, "Did you see those guys? What in hell are we in for?"

We took off again. Next stop, Vietnam. The mood on the airplane became somber. I looked around and picked up on the fear that these young men were feeling. The time was now at hand. Everything we had trained for; every fear we had imagined or denied, every hope that this moment would never come, was happening now. The truth was now coming fast. Could we take it? Would it be possible to get through this? Could we survive and make it home alive? The plane swung southwest and down over the South China Sea as it made its way to the southern shores of Vietnam.

The American Dream was over.

PART TWO:

VIETNAM

CHAPTER FIFTEEN

Vietnam

"GET OUT, GET OUT! MOVE, MOVE! GET YOUR ASSES OFF THIS PLANE NOW!!!"

I came to the open exit side door. I was hit by the heat, like a blast furnace. Next thing I knew, I was on the ground. Running. Running toward a bunker. Men were yelling. The jet's engines roared as the pilot began moving the plane down the runway to make room for the next transport coming right up behind him. I found the bunker, sat on my duffle bag. Men were running around yelling. There was a horrible smell; jet fuel mixed with something else. Oil barrels cut in half, filled with American soldiers' shit, soaked in diesel fuel, were on fire all around us. It was getting dark. There was a continuous, loud sound of something like *whomp* coming from all around in the distance. Helicopter blades thudded everywhere as an intense fear consumed us all.

The plane that had delivered us idled on the runway. As soon as our flight deplaned, they rapidly reloaded it with another two-hundred or more troops who were leaving Vietnam. With amazing speed and efficiency, its doors were slammed shut and it quickly taxied down the runway, kicked in its afterburners and took off at another steep angle, disappearing into the distance. I was on the ground in a completely different world; an unimaginably insane world of pain and suffering.

They ordered me onto a bus, filled with guys I'd travelled with on the plane. Most were like me, young soldiers. We were known as "Cherries" or "FNGs" (Fuckin' New Guys). Fear was pronounced and everywhere. Panic was palpable. The bus approached the main gate, guarded by heavily-armed military police who opened it and waved us through. We then drove off into the dark, heading for some place called the 90th Replacement Company. We had an MP gun Jeep with a soldier standing behind a machine gun, riding in front of us, and another behind us. The window frames on the bus, which held no glass, were screened by welded-on chain link fencing. Someone said that this was to prevent enemy grenades from being thrown into the bus. An older, grizzly looking, returning vet, cynically barked out that that these screens were useless, because "Charlie" (the word soldiers used for the Viet Cong or "the Enemy") had learned to attach hooks to their grenades. We'd all be blown away, anyway.

We drove through the slums of a city called Biên Hòa (pronounced *-been wha*), to get to the 90th Replacement Company. Through the darkness, I got my first look at how Vietnamese people lived. It was a wretched, dimly lit, hot, foul-smelling slum. The signs of war damage were everywhere; buildings blown up, bullet-ridden walls, rubble on the ground. It was evening and throngs of families were outside of their sweltering huts and dwellings, sitting and crouching by the roadside, cooking their meals under lamps, socializing at the end of the day. Many wore traditional Vietnamese conical peasant hats. The torn-up, narrow, winding, road swelled with pedestrians, bicycles, rickshaws, and all kinds of noisy, back-firing vehicles as well as military vehicles; the combined exhaust fumes were chokingly bad. It impressed me that these were an ancient people, historically forced into a new and foreign kind of life before they were ready.

Our armed motorcade trudged along slowly; our bus was loaded with fresh young troops who were picking up on the feeling - the *expectation* - that something terrible could happen at any moment. After about an hour, we arrived at our destination–the 90th Replacement Company. More armed guards checked us over, then opened the gates as we drove through into the dark.

We were ordered off the bus and immediately marched to the Company's Headquarters building where we stood at attention for a while before being relieved to stand at ease. We stood for some time until our names were called out by a Company Sergeant. Once all present and accounted for, we were given a brief description of where we were and what to expect until we received our replacement orders. Each one of us had already been assigned and promised to specific Army units all over South Vietnam. There were about 550,000 US soldiers serving in Vietnam during this time, split up amongst hundreds, maybe thousands, of various commands. Commonly during that part of the war, a soldier's tour was one year. He would then be rotated back to the US and reassigned from there. As a soldier left the war, another would be there to replace him. We were the fresh replacements. The 90th was a hot, dirty, humid, trashy, temporary place to transit through. We were told they would not figure our orders out until morning, so we should try to get some sleep until then. There were several barracks there and I found a cot with a filthy mattress, but it was impossible to sleep.

Reveille was called early that morning at the 90th

Replacement, and we all fell out into formation. They directed our attention to a large, garage-like structure and we were told to go in there and find the units we were going to be sent to. We were to find our names listed on sheets pinned to its bulletin board walls. First you had to locate the list that contained your MOS (Military Occupation Service) then you had to search that list for your name and military serial number. They arranged the names in alphabetical order, from top to bottom. My MOS was 91 A, Medical Corpsman. I found the list easily enough. Scrolling from the top down, I saw that those Army medics whose last names began with A, B, and C were, on that day, going to go to the 101st Airborne Division. This was a group of about twenty-five soldiers. I thought, *Poor bastards, many of them will die with the 101st.* They'd drawn a wavy pencil line under the C's, the D's, the E's, and the F's, who were going to go to the 25th Infantry Division. This was another notoriously dangerous division where a combat medic's chances were not great either. Then I came to the G's. The G's were in a category by themselves. There were only five soldiers in that category that day. Under the G's was scrawled another wavy pencil line separating the G's from the H's, and the rest of the alphabet. The G's were going to go to a unit called "The 44th Medical Brigade." And there I was listed! *Private E1 James Simpson Gibson,* right there in the middle of the list.

I nearly blanked out with gratitude and practically fell to the ground and kissed it as I suddenly realized I had been saved - blessed with great fortune! It was a miracle. While in Medics School at Fort Sam Houston, I had heard about the 44th Medical Brigade and had hoped that by some miracle, by some kind of intervention, or twist of fate, they would assign me to that unit. The 44th ran most of the Army's hospitals and provided many of the Army's other medical needs. Standing there that morning, I felt for sure that someone, something, was watching over me and guarding me. A sense of great relief came over me.

CHAPTER SIXTEEN

The 584th Ambulance Company

IT WAS EARLY morning and the 90th Replacement Company area was alive with buzzing activity. Orders were being handed out and directions given. Thousands of soldiers were processed. It was a madhouse of trucks, buses, and jeeps coming and going at a frantic pace. My small group who were being sent to the 44th Medical Brigade, waited at a particular location for a truck to pick us up and take us to our new unit.

An Army Three-Quarter truck with two helmeted drivers soon pulled over and they told us to throw our duffel bags in the back and jump in. We were off. We went out the gates of the 90th and then directly through the gates of an adjacent base, known as Long Binh Post. It was a surprise when only about ten minutes later, the truck stopped, the drivers got out and said, "Okay, get out. This is it, your new home! The 584th Medical Ambulance Company!"

I had been assigned to the 584th Medical Ambulance

Company, of the 58th Medical Battalion, of the 68th Medical Group, of the 44th Medical Brigade. Apparently, I would drive an ambulance for the next year for the 584th, which, stationed right there in Long Binh (pronounced–*long been*), was one of the largest Army bases in Vietnam. They led us into the 584th's Company Headquarters, where each of us reported in, stating our name, rank (I was a bottom level Private E1), and serial number. They assigned me to the 2nd Platoon and introduced me to its leader, Sergeant First Class Adams, who then led me to the 2nd Platoon's "Hooch."

Hooch's were small prefab, thin, aluminum buildings which housed most of the soldiers on the larger bases. At twenty feet wide and forty feet long, each could sleep about twenty men. They had only screened windows, no glass. Sandbags were stacked neatly and evenly, up against each hooch's exterior walls, at a height of about four feet, with the same width. There were four-foot gaps in the sandbags allowing for the front entrance and the back exit.

Sergeant Adams introduced me to some of the guys in the platoon, pointed to a mosquito net-covered cot, then told me to take off my boots, get in the cot, and get some sleep. I hadn't slept in days, so I passed out immediately. By the luck of the draw, I had escaped the worst. I really thought I was going to be sent straight into the field to a unit where the odds were high they would send me back home in a body bag before I'd had a chance to step off the bus. Being sent to the 584th in a rear area was a miracle.

I don't know how long I slept. It was probably something like twenty hours. When I awoke it at about 10 am, I looked around to see where I was. Getting there had been a blur. I sat up on the cot, drew back the mosquito netting, and placed my feet on the ground. As I was rubbing the sleep from my eyes and yawning awake, a guy came over and said, "Hi. We let you sleep all day yesterday and all night, because we knew how bushed you were by the transit in getting here. "Welcome." He seemed like a nice guy.

Soon, Sergeant Adams entered the hooch and arranged for a few guys to show me around the company area and help me get familiar with the place. First, we went to the Headquarters hooch where I briefly met the Company First Sergeant and the Company Commander. From there, they took me across a field to the battalion Mess Hall. An Army Mess Hall, or Chow Hall, is where soldiers stand in line to get their meals. While walking across the field, I heard a loud noise and looked up to see a cargo plane flying close to the ground just over my head. It was spraying a mist from its wings and I was almost immediately covered with a sticky film of something. Somebody told me they regularly sprayed the base like this to kill any plants growing around the base. It was a defoliant. Many years later, I learned that what they were spraying on us was a solution known as Agent Orange; used extensively in Vietnam as an herbicide, it also contained Dioxin, one of the most dangerous cancer-causing chemicals.

We ate chow then headed for the company Motor Pool. This was a yard where the 584th's ambulances and other vehicles were stored and maintained. It was there I received my first bit of serious advice about being in Vietnam. This came from a mechanic as a warning about what to think and what not to think while in Vietnam. This guy was an E4 (A "Spec 4" -four ranks up from basic Private E1) who was mostly in charge of the company's motor pool at the time; a red-neck, thick-neck, bigoted, piggish, kind of guy. He took us on a brief walk through the place, showed me the ambulances and other vehicles, and explained the mission of his motor pool. We were walking by the side of an ambulance when he suddenly stopped and pulled a large K-Bar knife from his web belt. He held its point close to my face, then plunged it well into a spare tire hanging from the door of an ambulance. He stared at me like he was looking through me and understood who I really was, and, like a bully, told me with a strong, white, southern drawl, "This is what will happen to *you* if we find out you're one of those Fuckin' cowardly Conscientious Objectors!"

I had gotten my warning.

December 8, 1968

Dear Mom and Dad ,

How are you today? There is not much activity here–nothing really newly significant– so this letter might be kind of hard to write.

Today, a Sunday, is my day off. It's not that I'll always have Sundays off, but that's just the way it happened this week. I Didn't really do a damn thing today and for that matter I haven't done a damn thing since I've been here. Things are down right boring.

|||

December 14, '68

Dear Mom and Dad

How are you tonight? I'm fine. Of course I'd rather be home but I shouldn't complain because things are worse for a lot of people

Wednesday evening, I started living on a different part of the base. I'm at a big supply depot about a mile or so from the main part of Long Binh. I live out here with one other guy – we share a tiny little room located in a one-story tin building which is the Headquarters building of the depot. We run an "Aid Station" out here for any injured workers– Vietnamese included. But actually we don't do anything of real significance because nobody will supply us with any medical supplies. So, we just give out band aids and run people into the hospital with our ambulance.

Reviewing my letters that I home sent to Mom and Dad from Vietnam, it's easy to see that I tried to make it sound as if everything was simply great for me in Vietnam. I didn't want them to worry any more than they already were.

584th Ambulances

Ambulances lined up facing company hooch's and a bunker

CHAPTER SEVENTEEN

The Depot

TEN DAYS AFTER checking into the 584th, Sergeant Adams told me to pack up my things because I was being shipped someplace else. He explained that our company had ground ambulance responsibilities at bases within a circumference of about seventy-five miles around the base of Long Binh. I was being sent out to relieve a medic at a two-man aid station with an ambulance at a huge supply depot on the eastern perimeter of our base. Soon an ambulance pulled in, I threw my stuff in the back, jumped into the shotgun seat and was off to another assignment.

The supply depot at Long Binh was one of the biggest the Army had in Vietnam; a massive complex of warehouses and other facilities that included what was the world's largest ammunition dump. All of this took up roughly the eastern half of the base of Long Binh. Those sixty-foot-high depot warehouses were stacked with metal storage containers known as Conexes, heavy corrugated, sealed, steel boxes, each about seven feet high, seven feet wide, and ten feet long. One Conex could weigh tons. The Conexes were stacked in immaculate rows about six or seven high, an equal number wide, and much more than that number deep within each warehouse. Other than aircraft, combat vehicles, and ammunition, they were the primary containers the military used in those days to ship just about everything to Vietnam for the war effort. The war materials, stored in thousands and thousands of Conexes, originating mostly from the US, came without end from the United States but also from markets the world over, into Vietnam from oceans spanning the globe, across the Pacific Ocean, up the Saigon River, aboard military and civilian cargo ships. "Sea Land" was the logo of the major US Corporation that contracted with our military to do most of this work. It was a gigantic US shipping corporation making huge profits in this evil game of war. The Sea Land logo could be seen everywhere on the ships at the docks in Saigon and on the hundreds and thousands of trucks going to and from Long Binh. A lot of the supplies and war materials also came in by air shipment offloaded from giant cargo planes that were constantly coming and going from the huge Air Force bases at Biên Hòa (Wah), near Long Binh (Been), and Tân Sơn Nhất (*Nute*), in Saigon. This was one of the biggest military logistical supply efforts ever attempted in American or global military history.

Vietnamese workers performed most of the manual labor done on the base of Long Binh. They were comprised mostly of women who made just pennies a day. They were our "Hooch Maids" who did our laundry by hand, spit-polished our combat boots, washed our sheets and cleaned and scrubbed our living quarters; who worked in our mess halls, cooked and served our meals, then washed our dishes, pots and pans. They did everything for almost nothing because the only alternative they had for their families was to starve to death. They also did most of the menial work at the depot.

Before sunrise, in the early morning hours, thousands of impoverished Vietnamese workers, mostly wearing their traditional conical bamboo hats, would show up at the base gates to see if we could let them in to perform a day of labor. Appointed Vietnamese labor bosses would look them over and select the ones they wanted, then load them up into buses and cattle trucks and carry them off to the different warehouse locations within the depot to go to work. My job at the depot was to man a simple aid station round the clock, and to stand by with an ambulance in case of emergencies.

CHAPTER EIGHTEEN

Living With a Psycho

SO THERE I was, living twenty-four hours a day, seven days a week, with a guy out at the depot on the farthest eastern perimeter of Long Binh Post. This would have been okay if the guy wasn't a complete psycho.

Zeke was from a small town somewhere in Pennsylvania. His major problem was that he had spent over a half of his one-year Vietnam tour serving as a combat medic with the First Infantry out in the field, and the war had knocked him off his rocker. This dude was wound up extremely tight. I first met him when he picked me up in Long Binh. While driving us out to the depot, he grabbed my hat off my head, threw it on the ambulance floorboard, and angrily told me hats weren't allowed in his ambulance. In that moment I knew this guy could be a problem.

Zeke was about as rude an asshole as you can imagine. He was right about everything and extremely critical of anything I said. I hated him immediately. He told me he had been in Vietnam for nearly a year and he was getting really Short. "Short" was the term soldiers used to mean that their tour in Vietnam was getting close to an end, and they would soon be going home. The date a soldier was expected to leave Vietnam was known as his "DEROS" date (Date of Expected Return from Overseas). It was then that he could fly back home on his "Freedom Bird." Zeke thought that since he had been in Vietnam for nearly a year, in comparison my experiences amounted to nothing.

We were stationed together in an office building at the depot in a room about the size of a large closet where we slept on cots within inches of each other. The office building was filled with officers and clerks during the day, but at night was deserted except for Zeke and me. At night when he would fall off to sleep, he would rapidly rub the inside of his left calf with the bottom of his right foot. He would also occasionally jerk spasmodically, jump up screaming and yelling out that he could not breathe. He had bad asthma and continuously sucked on an inhaler, wheezing loudly. It was damn near impossible to get any sleep.

Zeke would go on and on, vehemently, about how much he hated the Vietnamese people. He referred to them with the most derogatory racist epithets like, "Gooks," "Dinks" or "Slope Heads." He believed we should exterminate them. This guy was a creep with whom I had nothing in common. After living with him for about a week, we took a ride back into Long Binh and paid a visit to the 584th 2nd Platoon, our home platoon. That was when I had time to speak to the guy I had replaced out at the depot. He took me aside from the others where we could talk privately and asked me how it was living out there with Zeke. I sensed he wanted to tell me something. Right away we were talking about how completely nuts Zeke was. We both agreed Zeke was insane. He told me he had lived out there with him for several weeks but just couldn't take it anymore and had begged our platoon sergeant for a transfer back to the platoon. I was the sucker that'd ended up replacing him. So, Zeke and I drove our ambulance back out to the depot where I was stuck living with him. The days went by mostly with little incident. Soon I received a promotion to the rank of PFC, Private First Class (E3).

Christmas 1968 came and went.

Dec. 31, 1968

HAPPY NEW YEAR!
Dear Pop....
How's everything? I heard from Becky today.... she told me about Grandpa [Grandpa Carper's death]. I sure hope that Grandma comes through it okay. How are you feeling now Dad? Mom wrote a few days ago and told me that you were not feeling well at all and didn't want to leave you to go to Denver. How has Mom been Dad?
Has Becky had her kid yet? (Chrissy) Man. I'll bet she's getting fat.......
Time is going pretty fast... today I've been here for a month.

It was January 1, 1969, and I had survived the first month of my tour of duty in Vietnam. How had it been for me? Though I was grateful for my situation, I nevertheless lived in a continuous heightened state of fear. It was a hot, stinking, strange place. I had to live out there with nobody at all around except this crazy asshole.

The sights and sounds of war, especially at night, reminded me how tenuous everything really was. The base's eastern perimeter, where I was located, was comprised of a defense barrier known as a "berm." This was a ten-foot-high dirt-wall mound that ran for miles around the base. We slept in, and operated out of, a building inside and near the berm. It sat by itself, completely unprotected from enemy fire, on a slight hill, looking down at a string of machine-gun nests that were evenly spaced on the berm about seventy-five yards from each other. Looking out from the berm were many obstacles for the enemy to overcome if he wanted to come in. The defoliated and cleared field beyond the berm, for a distance of about a hundred yards, was loaded with row after row of mines, booby traps and listening devices, trip flares, and line after line of the deadly Concertina Wire spread out from rolls, with coils and coils of razor-sharp blades, ready to slice to death anything that tried to crawl over or through them. Beyond the berm and the perimeter defenses was the jungle, which was Charlie's domain. The machine-gun nests were sand-bagged bunkers that sat on and above the berm. Each nest was manned by a team comprising three riflemen and one machine gunner. The riflemen had M14 and M16 automatic rifles and the machine gunner commanded an Army M60 7.62 Caliber Machine Gun. The men also had controls to detonate the horrifically effective "Claymore Mines" if need be.

A Claymore Mine looks like a 16-inch, curved green brick. It's about three and a half inches thick. It sits up with its curve facing outward, about four inches above the ground, on two pairs of spikes. It's loaded with hundreds or thousands of small steel ball bearings, all enmeshed within a mold of plastic high explosive. Its back plate is made of solid steel. Upon detonation, a Claymore Mine clears and destroys just about everything within a 90-degree arch in front of it for a distance of about thirty-five yards. They connected the mines to the machine-gun nests, and their detonators, by wires. They were placed facing outwards at various strategic points within the perimeter. Besides their rifles, machine guns, and manual claymore detonators, the men also had grenades, spotlights, flares, and communications radios. Occasionally Charlie would probe our perimeter just to test us with a few incoming mortar rounds, in the general vicinity of our perimeter. The Viet Cong and the North Vietnamese forces could easily send thousands of soldiers to overwhelm our line of defenses at any time if they thought they found a weakness. It was a pretty thin line we had, and all this kept everybody awake and alert all night.

Nighttime was alive with the scenes and sounds of death. Tremendous explosions echoing in from near and far, lighting up the jungle. The incoming and outgoing artillery and the sound of small-arms fire going off here and there were continuous. Lines of arching red tracers lit the night and rained down from helicopters and other aircraft. Jet aircraft dove from high, dropped their thunderous loads, then shot back up into the sky and out of sight. Occasionally a flare would go up from our perimeter line, dangling for minutes at a time from a small parachute, lighting everything up like it was daytime, casting weird moving shadows. A machine gunner would open fire on whatever they thought or imagined they saw or heard. From the hill where I was stationed, I could clearly see, night after night, the war all around me. I had a bird's-eye view.

To get away from Zeke and his insanity, I would often walk out at night to the berm and sit on it for hours, looking outward. I felt better there by myself. I also felt incredibly alone. This was when I understood, really for the first time in my life, the importance of what my family meant to me. They meant *everything*. Mom and Dad had given me life and had loved and raised me, my brothers, and sister. They had sacrificed all that they had to do this, in the best way they knew how. I thought a lot about my dad, a World War II Veteran, who had experienced horrible things during that war. He had been difficult and sometimes disrespectful to me because of my opposition to the Vietnam War. Now there I was, on the other side of the Earth in another war and I began to understand him much better. I realized that if I should die in Vietnam, it would be my family who would truly suffer. I had many good friends at home, and they might miss me for a while, but after I was gone, I would eventually be forgotten as their lives went on. It would be a different thing for my family.

Before being sent to Vietnam, I'd thought I would never pick up a weapon to kill. I was an idealistic pacifist, and very much opposed to the Vietnam war, and had done all that I could to become a medic so I could work there in a position to save and not take lives. I could not imagine myself ever killing anyone. So far, I had not tested my idealism. This, however, was about to change. One late afternoon, after the staff had left the building Zeke and I lived in, we were kicking back in boredom on our cots within the sweltering closet we occupied there within the office building. Suddenly, an unbelievably loud explosion almost blew out my eardrums. Shock waves from the explosion reverberated through my body. It was the loudest and most frightening thing I'd ever experienced and was followed by several similar explosions that shook the building with terrific force.

Zeke's eyes went big as saucers and, in a panic, he jumped up and started screaming at the top of his lungs, "Get out! Get out, Man! Get your rifle and get out! This is incoming! Charlie is coming in right now! Get your rifle! Get out now! Charlie is coming in!"

There was no time to think. My survival instincts took over, and I grabbed up my M14 Rifle, which was loaded with a clip of ammo. I locked and loaded it and ran at full speed, in total, all-consuming fear, desperately following a screaming Zeke down the building's hallway, out the doorway. We both, with our rifles in hand, launched headfirst into a muddy trench located just outside the building's door. I was ready for anything! Out of nowhere, I was standing there, waist deep in, and covered in mud, with my rifle cocked, ready to blow away anything or anybody that was going to mess with me. We sloshed around in the mud for several seconds, wondering where Charlie was, when we heard the sound again.... but there was no impact from the explosion. Zeke laughed hysterically. His hands went up in relief and he laughed like the madman he was. I didn't know what to think. He looked at me strangely and screamed out, "Shit Man! This is outgoing! It is outgoing, you stupid shit! Now just look at you with your rifle, you idiot!"

One of the first things I realized after landing in Vietnam was that it was especially important to learn how to distinguish the difference between the sounds of "Incoming" fire, and "Outgoing" fire. This barrage that had scared the shit out of me was, thankfully, Outgoing fire. Without our knowledge, an artillery unit had been set up, just a hundred yards away from us, where we couldn't see it, and started to test fire its big guns, letting loose a horrific barrage. They fired the deafening rounds right over our heads, while we'd been quietly kicking back on our cots. We got into our ambulance and drove to our company headquarters in Long Binh, where we washed off the mud, cleaned up the mess and drove right back to the depot.

That night I once again returned to the berm and sat for a long time. I thought, repeatedly, about what I had done and how weak I was. That day I betrayed all I thought I was. I had agreed to go to Vietnam under my personal promise that I would never pick up a weapon to kill another man. The reality of my weakness stunned me to my core. I had failed the test right away. I became unbelievably depressed by this. I had instinctively picked up my rifle to kill. I'd never thought I would do this. It was then that I reassessed who I really was. I understood that nothing else really mattered other than my own personal survival. To hell with all the idealism. Principles be damned. I was no better or worse than anybody else here.

Just get through it, Jim! Just get home. I did not start this stupid fucking war. I wanted nothing to do with it, but they ordered me to go against my wishes. I have never wanted to harm anyone, but I'll do whatever I have to do to survive and stay alive and get home.

From that point on, I gave it no more thought and went nowhere without my rifle. I was ready to kill anybody or anything.

CHAPTER NINETEEN

Taking Control

MY HUMBLING REALIZATION transformed my internal identity. I had changed. I moved into a more protective, selfish mode. Something I hadn't known I was capable of before was now in me and exerting itself. I had probably been out there at the depot with the crazy man for about a month. Zeke was gradually wearing me down and I could not stand any longer his incredibly disrespectful, abusive, and threatening attitude towards me. He thought he was tough because of his stint out there in the bush with the First Infantry.

I thought, *Fuck this guy! He's got to go.*

When I was first ordered to go out to team up with Zeke I'd only been in the country for less than two weeks. He'd been in the war for about ten months-- a long time in a war zone. You can learn a lot in that length of time. By that time, you're a war veteran. I was green, choked with fear, and didn't understand what to expect or how to handle myself in Vietnam. I was unsure of myself in this terrifying place, and he took full advantage of my fear and inexperience. He had been having an excellent time humiliating me and making life tough for me. He was a sadist and having a great time at that. Zeke was a bully. I suspected he had probably been drawn off the line with the First Infantry and sent back to the rear because he couldn't handle it out there. A mentally unfit chicken-shit who was unstable as hell, he finally got me to where I'd had enough of his shit, so I started giving him some of my shit.

This guy had to go.

I began by not speaking to him or acknowledging him. I gave him more than the usual silent treatment. I just voided his existence out of my consciousness altogether; like he didn't even exist. He would say something, and I wouldn't answer or respond. At first, he got angry and threatened, but I kept my focus with no let-up. I was so successful using this strategy that, after a while, I really could not hear or see him at all. This went on for days, twenty-four hours a day. He got agitated as, little by little, I watched him disintegrate. It was fun watching him melt down. Now it was I who was getting to *him*. Things continued on like this for about another week until he finally broke and announced to me he'd had enough and was going to ask Sergeant Adams for a reassignment back to the base and the platoon, just to get away from me. He couldn't stand it anymore because I was driving him crazy. My game had worked! I won! It was easier than I'd thought it would be. Zeke, the asshole, loaded up his duffle bag full of his shit and we drove off in the ambulance back into Long Binh and the platoon. I happily dropped him off, and it was done. Thank God!

Upon arrival, they introduced me to his replacement who would ride back to live with me at the depot where I would now be in charge. His name was Kent, an enormous baby Huey kind of guy, gentle and innocent, but really kind of thick and dumb. He was about nineteen years old, from the lower classes of Boston. He had huge clumsy hands, was uncoordinated, toothless, and had one continuous thick eyebrow which spread across his forehead; sort of like what one might imagine a Neanderthal to look like. He spoke with that really funny kind ethnic Bostonian accent where "You go to the baw, to get a bee-ah." His favorite litterateur was found in comic books. I thought, *Oh Great. How am I ever going to relate to this gentle, yet uneducated, dumb, grown child?*

But I was happy and knew that anything would be better than Zeke. We headed out to the depot. I was now the man in charge of our two-man detail. As time went by, I got used to Kent, with his childish ways, and we passed the days in the heat and boredom with almost no serious incidents which would require our help. I worried a lot because Kent seemed almost incapable of handling just about anything. What if something were to come up that required someone whom I could depend upon and trust to save my life?

CHAPTER TWENTY

Cornbread Girlfriend

WE GOT A call to respond to a life-threatening situation at the north-east perimeter of the base, a few miles from our location. A soldier was convulsing and unable to breathe. We jumped into our ambulance and sped out toward the depot's massive junkyard that was way out there some place.

This junk yard was huge, and it took a while to find the unit where the supposedly dying soldier was located. A gigantic stockpile of mountains of old, worn-out tires, tank treads, and anything else you could imagine the wastes of war to be, it was all stacked dozens of feet into the air, as far and wide as the eye could see. It was a VC infiltrator's dream, which took up square miles of space. Small, dark alleyways crisscrossed throughout its dark, and deeply layered, confusing, labyrinth. I had seen nothing like it.

We found the Logistics Company's Headquarters' hooch, and the soldier who was lying on his back on a cot. I checked his pulse and his chest to see if he was breathing. His pulse was weak, and breathing was close to nil. I searched for wounds of any type but spotted none. I began CPR. This meant mouth-to-mouth breathing, alternating with deep compressions of his sternum to simulate a heart rhythm, as I'd been trained to do during medic's school. I told Kent to go out to the ambulance and get a stretcher. While continuing CPR, we got the soldier loaded and into the back of the ambulance. With Kent driving, we took off for the 93rd Evacuation Field Hospital in Long Binh. It was a long and bumpy ride getting back into Long Binh as I kept up CPR all the way. The roads were comprised of dried caked mud, extremely rutted, causing me to bounce all over the back of the ambulance. Between breaths and chest compressions, I yelled out to Kent the directions to the hospital.

Upon approaching the gate to the base and the hospital, I realized this guy might die and we didn't have time to stop and let the MP guards search us. I yelled out to Kent, "Just run the God-Damned gate! Don't stop!"

Kent did this, even though I expected machine-gun bullets to come ripping into the backsides of the ambulance, the guards didn't shoot us. We backed into the 93rd's emergency dock and brought the guy into the Emergency Room on a gurney. An ER Doc took over right away as I stood to the side. The Doc checked him over and injected a drug using a long needle straight through the man's chest and into his heart. He waited and watched the guy for a bit, then did something that really surprised me. He punched the guy strongly and sharply in the chest, with his right-hand knuckle. Right away the soldier's eyes sprang wide open, and I realized there was something going on here I did not understand. This guy was faking it. Suddenly this comatose-appearing soldier was wide awake and responsive to questioning. In a little time, the Doc got it out of him that he'd eaten rat poison. This was a clear attempted suicide. The Doc looked over at me and I explained to him

I had performed mouth-to-mouth resuscitation on him all the way into the hospital. He told me I probably had saved the soldier's life, then turned to the soldier and said comically, "Meet your new girlfriend."

After thoroughly rinsing my mouth out with mouthwash, I spent the next few hours pumping the guy's stomach to remove the rat poison from his system. I asked the soldier how he had come to eat rat poison? He was a very childlike, country hick, who made up a ridiculous story that went something like this:

"Well, I was there taking cover inside of one of our bunkers out there at the depot junk yard and was getting kind of hungry. I saw what looked like cornbread, stuffed inside a cardboard toilet paper roll right there on the floor of the bunker, so I ate it."

He didn't want to admit it. We all knew what those little cardboard rolls, in the bunkers, filled with yellow rat poison were. Who knows what he'd experienced in the war to have led him into such a depression to kill himself? He had tried to end it all, but I had screwed up his plan. Kent and I drove back out to the depot.

Poor dude. I felt sorry for him.

CHAPTER TWENTY-ONE

A Lesson for
the Day

WE RECEIVED A desperate call that there had been a terrible accident at one of our warehouses, involving many injuries. We ran out, jumped into the ambulance and drove to the scene. Upon arrival, I could immediately tell something horrible had happened. There were two or three large crowds of Vietnamese peasant women outside one of our vast warehouses. Women were screaming, tearing at themselves, wailing in misery. They were writhing in horrible mental anguish.

"*Choi oye..Choi oye....*"

They were out of their minds with an incomprehensible, uncontrollable kind of loss and grief.

I got out of the ambulance with my aid bag dangling from my shoulder and approached the first group of hysterical women. They cleared the way for me, and I saw the damage right away. A young American warehouse worker, a soldier, came up to me shaking, and explained what had happened. He'd been working on a huge forklift in the warehouse and had lost control.

That morning, these Vietnamese women had been humbly

going about their duties with their little hand brooms whisking away the red dirt and dust from under and around the massive stacks of Conexes, when suddenly from above, one stack gave way and came crashing down upon them. Three or four women were instantly crushed to death. A dozen others laid about with life-threatening injuries. Those who survived, upon realizing what had happened to their loved ones, went into a state of something known as "Wailing." I'd heard of this before but never seen it. It's the expression of deep uncontrolled sorrow and misery – the expression of the most immense kind of human suffering.

"Choi oye..Choi oye.... Choi oye..Choi oye.... Choi oye..Choi oye...."

They were going crazy in grief. It was a nightmare scene. I separated the dead from the injured and assessed the situation, paying attention to those whose injuries seemed most life threatening. Many of them were bleeding and had multiple fractures. A few were barely breathing. By this time, a crowd of onlookers had surrounded the scene to observe; mostly Army soldiers working there at the depot. I asked them to help me, first by bringing out the four folding stretchers I carried onboard the ambulance. We unfolded them on the ground. Then I directed them to help me place the most injured on the stretchers. After frantically dressing a lot of bleeding wounds and applying several splints to broken bones, we packed the injured women into the ambulance and took off immediately, driving as a fast as I could for the 93rd Evac in Long Binh. Within about twenty minutes, I arrived at the 93rd and quickly backed the ambulance into the emergency area where the medics on duty assisted me in offloading and carrying these injured women into the emergency room.

Right away I noticed the sour disappointed expressions

on the medics' faces. When I brought the women into the ER there was a great commotion as the medical staff immediately sprang into action to save and attend to these people. But upon the realization that I had brought in only Vietnamese, and not Americans, their attitudes changed. Their disappointment was obvious. Some of the staff turned their heads in disgust and uttered obscenities. They were pissed that they had to work on these Vietnamese women. It appalled me. I'd completed my responsibilities as far as I was concerned. I'd brought these women who had been seriously injured in one of our warehouses, into one of our hospitals for treatment. As I was folding up my stretchers and preparing to leave the hospital, a senior Non-Commissioned Officer, an Army lifer in charge of the 93rd's Emergency Room, approached me. He was a stern-looking older lifer who carried a lot of weight around that hospital.

He gave me a chewing out – "Private Gibson. Never bring your fucking gooks in here again! Do you hear me!? Do you understand me!?"

I responded, "Yes Sergeant, I hear you, but what was I supposed to do with them?"

"FUCK! Drop them off on the side of the road somewhere, for all I care, shoot 'em, but never bring this shit in here again!"

"But Sergeant, we injured them out at the depot!"

"That doesn't mean shit. You've got your warning!"

That was my lesson for the day. I went back to the ambulance and drove Kent and I back out to our depot aid station. When we got there, we scrubbed the stretchers and washed out the back of the ambulance. It was a disgusting mess of human blood, piss, shit, and vomit. I never found out how many of the women we carried into the 93rd that day lived or died. This was how the poor people, the Vietnamese people, whom America was there supposedly to protect and defend, were treated. I was, from then on, to learn repeatedly this horrible lesson. What I had seen that day was no aberration.

January 27, 1969

Dear Mom and Dad,

Well, another week has gone by– uneventful as usual. We have had a little more business this week, though. Mostly minor cases involving the "Nationals" who work out here at the depot.......

24th Feb. 1969

Dear Mom and Dad

...... Not much happening here. There has been a little bit of stepped up activity in and around Saigon during the past few days but there isn't anything to worry about here.

*"Hooch Maids," on their way to work
at the depot in Long Binh.*

CHAPTER TWENTY-TWO

Tet Offensive – 1969

IT WAS THE 22nd of February and the "Tet," Vietnamese Lunar New Year Celebration of 1969, was at hand. It was the close of a quiet evening at the depot when we were preparing to call it a day and hit the sack. Suddenly there was a knock on the door of the aid station. It was a Sergeant from one of the depot's warehouses who presented us with one of his night workers. He was an old Vietnamese man, a "Papa San," who was complaining of serious pain in his abdominal area. The Sergeant dropped him off with us and left. Papa San was grabbing his stomach and crying out with a distorted expression of pain on his face....

"*Beaucoup Dao!*" ('terrible pain') "*Oh, 'Choi Oye!... Beaucoup Dao... Beaucoup Dao...*'"

We weren't doctors, just medics, with only a basic knowledge of medical care. We gave the old man some antacid and hoped this would calm him down. He became even more animated with his demonstrations of horrible pain, so after about an hour of this, we took him down to the 93rd Evac, to have him examined and see what they could do for him. We got to the 93rd at about 11:30 that night and took the old man into the ER, hoping the asshole Sergeant who had previously warned me about bringing Vietnamese into his ER would not be on duty. Luckily, he wasn't. A sympathetic doctor there diagnosed and cared for the old man, and I went over to a bench to relax.

It was about midnight when I heard what sounded like someone knocking hard on the Quonset hut roof of the Emergency Room. It started off with a few knocks, then increased in rapidity until it became almost a steady drumbeat of knocking. This went on for a minute until a soldier, one of the medics there, came running into the ER and shouted out, "We're being attacked! The base is under attack! Missiles are coming in! It's Incoming! It's Incoming!"

I stepped outside to see for myself. It was true; the base was being attacked and there was a fire fight just about seventy-five yards from where I stood. One of our machine-gun nests opened up and was firing on, and spraying bullets to the other side of the highway just outside the base perimeter. There was also fire being let loose from the rifles of our guards. Red tracers were blazing everywhere. I stayed outside long enough to hear load explosions coming from many directions around the base simultaneously.

The base was under attack.

There was something about Papa San that made me suspicious. Could he have known that the base was going to be attacked that night at midnight? I figured he did. I noticed that right after the attack began; he sat up straight and, like magic, all of his symptoms seemed to have suddenly gone away. This told me everything. The old man knew. He just wanted to get the hell out of the depot area because he'd probably heard, through the underground, that the VC might come through there to assault the base.

Alarms were sounded and the hospital immediately went into its lock-down emergency mode to accept mass casualties. My partner and I grabbed Papa San and got him the hell out of there. We took him out to the ambulance and told him to hide in the back. Hell was breaking loose, all around us. Tremendous explosions rang out in the distance, at the depot and at other locations around the base. Kent and I wondered what we should do. We had no comm radio, so we drove back to our company headquarters at the 584th, which was near the 93rd Evac, to await instructions. I drove into the company area in the dark without headlights and parked it directly in front of the 584th Headquarters hooch, right next to about a half dozen ambulances waiting to take off. We'd told Papa San to lie down in the back of the ambulance and hide. I was afraid that if any of my fellow soldiers saw him, they would have killed him.

The company stirred with activity. Calls came into the desk from several locations around the base for help with the wounded. It was now half past midnight. Ambulances rolled out. Kent and I walked over to the 2nd platoon to talk with Sergeant Adams. He told us to standby. So we hung around the 2nd Platoon hooch in the dark, with the other guys, watching the horrifying scene all around us. We waited for our turn to be called out.

It looked to me that where we had come in from, just about an hour before, out at the depot, was under a major attack. I could see huge fireballs followed by thunderous explosions coming in from out there. I thought, *Wow, thank you Papa San!*

In the beginning, the attacks seemed to come from several locations surrounding the perimeter of Long Binh. Explosions of incoming mortars and rockets, and machine gun and small arms fire, were going off all about. All but one of these attacks were diversionary attacks meant to confuse and throw off our base defense forces. After about an hour and a half, we realized where the actual attack was going to come from. It was also clear what it was hoping to accomplish—to destroy the US Army Headquarters in Vietnam.

The United States Army commanded its war in Vietnam from its Headquarters buildings in Long Binh. Large two-story prefabricated aluminum office buildings, on a hill, close to and looking down at the base's southern perimeter defenses, made up the Command. During the day they were stuffed with Generals and other officers and clerks as they ran the war for the Army. At night, the buildings stood empty, except for a few guards. Just a short distance from the Headquarters, buildings were the personal billets of many Generals and other high-ranking officers who ran the war. They lived like petty kings with special luxurious private compounds; air-conditioned mobile homes staffed with servants, prostitutes, and more. They had more than the comforts of home. Each General and Colonel also had his own ring of defenses surrounding his personal compound, manned round-the-clock by heavily armed MPs.

On the night of February 23, 1969, the North Vietnamese Army and the Viet Cong launched their attack on US Army Headquarters, Long Binh. I am sure their mission was not only to overrun its defenses and destroy it, but to at least deliver a message to the Army's Generals and staff that they were not safe there. They were not safe, even within the perimeter of Long Binh.

The enemy attack was intense. First, they let loose with a barrage of mortar and missile fire. Next, they advanced using suicide squads. About a dozen, wearing explosive satchels strapped to their bodies, emerged seemingly from nowhere, coming from hiding places just beyond our perimeter defenses. They ran straight ahead into a hail of our gunfire. They threw themselves at our first line of concertina wire defenses, igniting themselves and blowing up the first line. This created a hole that the next suicide squad ran through. They did the same thing to our next line of defenses. They kept doing this until a suicide squad made it to our berm line and overran a few of our machine-gun nests, killing or wounding many.

Our base guard command had arranged it so that there were literally hundreds of Army soldiers lined up shoulder-to-shoulder on the berm firing away at them. Our defense forces lit up the battle scene with flares dangling from parachutes. From where we were at the 584th, a few miles away, we could see and hear the ferocity of attack being waged. We watched as the night war lit alive with fire. Helicopter gunships went up and were soon hovering over the battle area in tight circles, unleashing a merciless downpour of red-hot lead from above. In rivers of red, the fate of the enemy was clear.

"Puff the Magic Dragon" soon made its appearance that night, circling over the area. Puff was a World War II-era, two-engine C47. It was a multi-purpose cargo plane that the Army had converted into an unbelievably effective battlefield gunship with two "Mini-Guns" mounted on its left side. Each Mini Gun could unleash up to two thousand rounds of machine gun fire a minute. The pilot directed his plane to a selected spot of suspected enemy activity, came in slow, dipped his left wing, and encircled it, and the gunners opened fire. Four thousand rounds per minute of machine gun fire sounded like a loud, horrible chain saw. It just annihilated anything and everything on the ground it fired upon. During the battle for Long Binh that night, Puff intermittently came and went. There was almost no defense against such a weapon. Besides the helicopter gunships and Puff, they also called in jet strikes to make matters even worse for the enemy. And yet, faced with such overwhelming firepower, the NVA and Viet Cong troops advanced and succeeded in overrunning and briefly occupying a few machine-gun nests that night. They breeched our perimeter and nearly attacked the Army Headquarters.

It turned out, however, to be a lopsided blood bath for the enemy, as we just had too much firepower for them to handle. They were wiped out. We killed hundreds of them that night. I stood by the 2nd Platoon area with Kent and other platoon medics throughout the night and the early morning hours. We were waiting to be called up, to go out to the battle area to pick up casualties. Crazy Zeke was there, roaming around and mingling amongst the group. My 2nd Platoon buddies, Jackson, and Kerrey, were called up. They were given orders and immediately took off in their ambulance towards the battlefront with their lights off. After about an hour, they returned. They parked and walked in silence back to where the rest of us were waiting in the dark. We had lots of questions for them. Zeke grabbed up a nearby folding chair, plunked it down in front of them, got in their faces, and interrogated and demanded information from them–

"Okay, what in the Fuck was it like out there? What did you see? What did you *do*?"

Jackson looked okay, but I could see that Kerrey was really shaken up by what he had seen. He was white as a ghost, frozen in fear and having difficulty speaking, like his throat had closed. Trembling, shaking, he blurted out:

"There was blood everywhere in the back of the ambulance. Lots of brains, lots of guts. I had blood all over my hands. Many bodies."

He couldn't go on. The experience had been too much for him and had done him in. He could not speak. It was obvious to the rest of us there was horror out there. We waited, with feelings of dread, for our turns.

In the meantime, I'd forgotten about the old man, Papa San, who I'd told to hide in the back of our ambulance. I went back over to check on him and he was gone. He had disappeared, and I never saw him again. Kent and I told no one about him. I think he may have been a VC spy.

The battle wore on.

After a few hours, they ordered Kent and me to take our ambulance out to a specific location at the front and report to an Army unit there. We had no radios or maps and no idea of how to find the unit. To make matters worse, we were under total Blackout conditions and had to turn our headlights off and drive in total darkness.

There I was, driving out there in the dark to find the unit. By this time, things seemed to calm down on the front. In the early morning hours, I drove the ambulance toward the south perimeter, where all the action had been taking place. It turned out to be an impossible mission. We had no idea where to go, so we just drove around in the general direction of the front, hoping to luck out and find any unit that might need our help. I drove around in the darkness for quite some time until I recognized men ahead. I momentarily turned on my headlights to see. Standing right in front of me, in full combat attire, was an Army Sergeant pointing his M16 directly at my head, I doused my lights immediately. He was threatening to kill us for exposing them with our lights and was irate and screaming at me. I yelled back at him:

"Hey Sarge, we've heard that you've taken casualties and we are here to evacuate them!"

This calmed him down a bit, and he told me that there were no casualties he knew of amongst the men in his area. I said, "Okay Sarge. We've got to be on our way now to find them!"

He let us pass and I felt lucky to have gotten out of that situation alive. He looked like he wanted to waste us. It was apparent that the night's battle was pretty much over, and I realized we would find nothing or do any good by driving around aimlessly in the dark, so I drove back to the company area.

We were all standing around, exhausted from the night's attacks, when, just before the sun rose, we heard a faint, yet deep rumbling noise. The rumbling grew louder and seemed to come toward us. As the minutes went by, its sound intensified until it was deafening. The ground I stood on rumbled. Then someone yelled out,

"Look! It's Patton's son!"

It was true! Suddenly, on the road just below our company area, came roaring a huge battle tank leading a squadron of smaller tanks. There was a tank commander striking an overly dramatic pose, standing in the tank's turret looking forward with arms folded, as his tank advanced. He was an Army Colonel, the son of the famous World War II tank commander, General George Patton, leading several tanks into Long Binh, to set up armored positions around the US Army Headquarters, securing it from further attack. The Tet Offensive of 1969, eventually to become known as "Mini-Tet," was a series of coordinated attacks conducted by units of the People's Army of Vietnam, which hoped to replicate the successes of their 1968 campaign that they waged the year before. It failed at this, but nevertheless conveyed their message to the American public about the seriousness of their intent to keep on fighting.

After we watched the tank parade that morning, with much trepidation, I drove Kent and myself back out to our assignment - the aid station at the depot. Even though the night before it had appeared that the depot had been hit hard and destroyed by incoming attacks, I could see that there was only minor damage. We settled back into our aid station and prepared for whatever was next. There was tension in the air as it was not clear to us just what "Charlie's" intentions were. It was at about seven hundred hours the next evening, while Kent and I were quietly engaged in a card game with a local MP, inside one of the depot's office buildings when the depot came under attack again. Right away we knew we had to get out of the building to survive. Kent and I made our way outside the building and headed for our aid station. We thought there could be casualties needing our help, and we wanted to be set up and ready to receive them as they came in.

We ran out in the dark towards our building. The field separating the building we had been playing cards in from the building that housed our aid station had become almost impassable. It was a barren field of red clay mud that had been heavily rained upon then dried, leaving nothing but deep pits, like concrete, to break your ankles upon in the dark.

The rockets came in, *Whoomp... Whoomp...*

Somehow, we made it to the door of our aid station. It was then I realized that we'd locked the door, and Kent had the keys. He started fumbling around with the keys as the incoming rockets with their enormous explosions began to "walk in," closer and closer to our position. It was then I protected my own life. I shouted out to him– "Take cover!"

I left Kent there at the door fumbling with the keys and ran as fast as I could to a road culvert, crawled inside, curled up about fifty feet away from the building. I jumped into the culvert just before I heard a tremendous explosion go off over my head. I was about three or four feet under the ground when it hit. I looked out to see white phosphorous chemicals raining down to the ground. That was a close one!

The rocket fire ceased, and I came out from underground to find Kent still alive and standing by the side of the aid station with a deer-in-the-headlights kind of expression on his face. Thankfully, he was okay. He was too stupid to realize that it had almost killed him right there. The last barrage was the last we heard from Charlie that night. We went in and laid on our cots and rested, but I could not sleep, expecting more to come.

Enemy action picked up during the next few days. The depot had been closed since the attacks began, and in the building next to our aid-station building, the Army's Long Binh Post Defense Command Headquarters, for its eastern perimeter, had been set up. This meant there were lots of high-ranking officers, Colonels, Light Colonels, Majors, etc., on duty with us, night and day. The Command officers wanted us medics to be constantly at their side in case they got hit; to hell with the guys on the berm whose lives were actually on the line protecting us. At night from the tree line, the VC would occasionally open up on the berm with mortars, machine gun and small arms fire. In return, our soldiers would fire back. Flares would light up the night and the war would go on. These officers with their phony sense of self-importance were pitiful. I thought most of them to be just chicken-shit, self-promoting corporate types using their Army careers as steppingstones.

A telling incident occurred one night. It was dark, and I was standing next to a Colonel and a Major. I was in my combat uniform with a steel helmet on, and a medic's aid-bag under my arm. Just then some minor fire came from the berm area and a flare shot up. The sound of this scared the shit out of the Colonel and the Major who ducked down to hide. I didn't even flinch. Having been out there for a few months, I'd grown accustomed to this kind of thing. It was nothing. I almost laughed out loud when they cowered. Our fearless officers!

But what really got to me after they'd recovered themselves; after they'd gotten back up from the ground and straightened their helmets; after almost shitting their pants in fear, I heard the Colonel blurt out something that really disgusted me. He turned to his aid, the Major, trying to impress him with his superior officer's bravery and knowledge, and said,

"You know Major, those boys out there on the line, they might smoke way too much pot and give us problems but when it really comes down to it, by God, they are damn good troops!"

Just then some more minor fire came in from the line again and the assholes were once again down on their hands and knees, quivering in fear.

|||

Hanging out at Headquarters, I could listen to the radios and hear the live broadcasts coming in from all around the base. These broadcasts were being called in from soldiers on the ground and were noticeably clear, dramatic, and easy to hear. There was a lot of violence. You could hear men screaming as gunfire and explosions were going off. The base continued to be attacked from several directions.

One night there was something happening out at the depot junk yard that stood out from the rest and really grabbed my attention. Earlier in this story I wrote about the "junk yard" and how it was a maze, a labyrinth, and a VC infiltrator's dream to get lost in. Over the radio, I listened to a horrible situation developing out there. The enemy had tunneled under the perimeter and come up into the junk yard loaded with weapons and explosive satchels. They had their way with our troops out there, blowing things up and killing them at will. Our warehouse soldiers working out there never really had a chance as they were being attacked by seasoned Viet Cong troops who knew what they were doing. I could hear our guys on the radio, just a few miles from us, screaming for help and mercy, then gunfire, followed by more screaming and explosions. Then deadly silence. After that there was nothing but the static of the radio and some vague sounds of movement.

No more communications from the junkyard. It was awful to realize that several men I'd met out there at the junkyard were now dead. I heard it live. Of course, the officers would not allow me to leave their side. I wondered if one of the guys killed out there at the junk yard that night was the guy I'd previously saved from his attempt to kill himself.

As the days and nights went by out at the depot, things gradually simmered down and the enemy's attacks backed off to the status quo. They shut the Defense Command Headquarters down and there were no more officers to bug me. However, boredom once again resumed as my major problem.

March 2, 1969

Dear Mom and Dad,

How are you this week? .... Tomorrow is the 3rd and will mark the 3rd month of my tour. Looking back over these months I can say that they haven't been too trying on me and I hope that the next 9 are as good. ....

Love, Jim

CHAPTER TWENTY THREE

Long Binh
Ambulance Stories

IT WAS THE second week of March 1969. I had been stationed at the depot for about two-and-a-half months. I'd gotten rid of crazy Zeke and survived and gone through so much, but I was really tiring of being out there alone with Kent. He was a nice guy and couldn't help it, but his simple, childlike mind as my only companion was getting to me. So, I'd asked Sergeant Adams for a rotation back to the Platoon, and he granted it.

It was good to be back to the 2nd Platoon again, where I at least had a choice of guys to hang out with. It was difficult for me though, because with just a few exceptions, I had little in common with the men there and it was hard to start up a conversation. They mostly liked the comic books and Playboy magazines you could get cheap at the PX. Mostly uneducated, working-class young guys, of all races, drawn from all corners of America, many were what Karl Marx once described as "The Lumpenproletariat"— the bottom of the barrel – devoid of any class consciousness. Some of them would have been sent to juvenile hall or prison if not for the draft, so they saw life in the Army as an opportunity. At least you might get three square meals a day.

The company assigned the 2nd Platoon to provide ambulance coverage for the 93rd Evacuation Hospital in Long Binh, which was within a few hundred yards of our company's headquarters. Our orders were to provide a two-man ambulance team to stand by outside the 93rd ER, twenty-four hours a day, seven days a week. We provided two ambulance teams who rotated this duty – twenty-four hours on, twenty-four hours off. I served on one team. The shift started after morning chow, when we would drive over to the 93rd and relieve the other crews standing by. When not out on a mission, we waited with our ambulances backed up to a ramp running from the ER's swinging entry doors straight out to a helipad about fifty yards away. When helicopters came in, we would rush out to greet them with gurneys, off-load the injured and the dead, then bring them into the emergency room.

We sat around and waited inside our stifling ambulances for something to happen. The heat and humidity were, at times, unbearable. The temp could rise to 120 degrees and the humidity to one hundred percent. We just had to sit there in misery and *wait*. Occasionally a Dust Off (Army air-ambulance) would come in and we would go out to off-load its contents. Sometimes it would be dead soldiers on stretchers with their blown-off limbs lying by their sides. More often, it would be soldiers still alive with grievous injuries, like sucking chest wounds. We brought them into the ER where the staff would spring into action to save them. Sometimes I heard our soldiers– most of whom were only boys - begging for their lives. I heard dying soldiers, old and young, cry out, "Mommy! Mommy! Please help me!"

War was disgusting. These experiences went on and on for days after day, seemingly without end.

|||

One night, I was ordered to transfer a gravely injured young soldier with a horrible head wound from the 93rd to the 24th Evacuation Hospital, also located at Long Binh. The 24th's specialty was the treatment of head and brain wounds. We rolled the patient out the swinging doors of the 93rd ER and transferred him to a stretcher to get him into our ambulance. We got him inside and I took on the role of the attending medic in the back while my partner drove. Soon after we left the 93rd, the soldier started flailing about in uncontrollable delirium and pulled out his IVs, ripping off his wound dressings. A gaping hole in the side of his head left him uncontrollable. One of his hands was hanging on by only a few strands of flesh. He was gushing blood from both wounds and screaming, out of his mind. He flailed his arm, and I was afraid his hand would be severed from his arm. It flopped about like a fish on a line, and I could hear the bones of his arm and wrist cracking. I tackled him to save him and became drenched in his blood as I attempted to restrain and care for him. It was a slippery mess. We got him to the 24th Evac where we transferred him. I don't know if he survived.

|||

Another night we got a call from the MPs that there was a man downed by a serious gunshot wound on the base. They gave us the company location and we responded immediately, driving off to find the company. It was always difficult finding anything at night in the dark at Long Binh, as we were always under blackout conditions. It was almost impossible to know where you were going, so I relied on memory, instinct, and intuition to get me where I needed to go at night. We found the unit. There were men with red flashlights waving, guiding us into the area. I parked the ambulance. A sergeant instructed me to follow him. It was dark and spooky, foreboding, feeling hung in the air.

"The medics are here! Clear the way."

When I entered the dimly lit tent, a senior NCO approached and said,

"I can't get a pulse on him!"

He pointed to a cot where a large Black soldier lay on his back wearing nothing but his green Army underwear shorts. I went to his side and saw he was motionless and not breathing. He had no pulse. With my fingers, I pried open his eyelids and saw that his pupils were unevenly dilated. Because of my medic's training, I immediately knew exactly what I was looking at and I responded to the NCO... so that all could plainly hear,

"You can't get a pulse on him because he's dead."

The men who silently stood around in the darkened tent that night with numb, stunned expressions on their faces listened and understood me. What they expected me to do, I didn't know. There was no saving this guy. But I had my job to do, so I decided I should at least try to find out what killed the man. It was a mystery. With all of them standing around, I knelt over the soldier from his right side and scanned his body from top to bottom, seeing no visible wounds. There was, however, an awful smell. I placed my right hand up and under his left shoulder and raised it a bit. There was a sucking sound as I did this and right away, I could see that he was lying in a pool of coagulated blood. I laid his shoulder back down, wanting to know where the blood had come from. I grabbed his head, behind his ears, and with both of my hands lifted it off of the pillow it rested upon.

What happened next was probably one of the worst things I saw in Vietnam. As I lifted his face up, the entire front of his head became separated from the back of his head and his white and red brains came spilling out onto the pillow and the floor below. Blood and body fluids dripped everywhere.

I heard someone utter, in the background, that a guy had placed a rifle muzzle into the man's mouth and fired as he slept. It had blown the back of his head off. That was all I needed to hear. I was really doing a grand act, trying to look so cool and all, as if nothing affected me and that I had everything under control. I ordered my partner to go out to the ambulance and bring back a folding stretcher. We unfolded it on the floor, next to the dead man's cot. I ordered four men standing about to each grab one corner of the sheet he was lying on, then counted: "one and two, and lift." They placed the body, blown out brains and all, onto the stretcher, and under my instructions, carried it out to the ambulance.

As I mentioned, there was a lot of blood and body fluids dripping everywhere. This probably also included parts of his brains. As they carried the stretcher out to the ambulance, dogs came running out of nowhere in the dark, and attempted to snap up to get to the dead body. They lapped at the blood, brains, and body fluids that were dripping off the stretcher. The body was in my ambulance, so I drove it to the 24th Evacuation Hospital in Long Binh, where we found a gurney and wheeled it into the ER. The night nurse on duty, working in a dimly lit room by herself, had practically no reaction when we wheeled in the corpse. She just told us to transfer it to a table in the room, and fill out some simple form that she handed to me. That was it. We left.

I learned later about how the murder happened. Apparently, the "Soul Brother" had, earlier that evening, been playing cards with some of his fellow Black comrades in their company's recreation room. When the card game ended, the brother went to his hooch, laid down on his back and went to sleep. Nothing was wrong. Nobody noticed anything. One of his fellow brothers he'd been playing cards with, went over to the company's armory and was able to check out his rifle, claiming he wanted to clean it. He then took his rifle into the hooch, stuck its muzzle into his buddy's mouth and fired a round, blowing out his brains.

After he did that, he calmly put down his rifle and walked over to his bunk just a few feet from where his brother laid dead. He then sat down on his bunk and took out a tobacco pipe, lit it and inhaled, smoking it as if nothing had happened. According to witnesses, no argument had taken place at the card game. There was no hint to anybody that there was any problem at all between the two. The murderer seemed to be surprised that he'd done anything wrong. He was taken into the 93rd Evac's Psych ward, deemed to be insane, and soon evacuated to the States.

The day after this experience I had a bit of a mental breakdown. My head began, strangely, to twitch from side to side. This uncontrollable twitching kept up for the next few weeks until I didn't notice it anymore.

|||

The 44th Army medical brigade ran a prisoner-of-war hospital in Long Binh. Its mission was to treat captured, injured, Viet Cong prisoners, before getting them well enough to transfer them down to a South Vietnamese military hospital in Saigon. The word was out that this South Vietnamese military hospital was also an interrogation center where prisoners might be interrogated, and tortured, sometimes to death, for information. One morning, Sergeant Adams ordered me to drive my ambulance to our brigade's POW hospital to be part of a convoy of company ambulances. The mission was to load up as many POWs as we could, then drive them down to Saigon.

The loading of the prisoners began. I had four wounded Viet Cong prisoners to load. Each had severe injuries. Three out of the four were in full body casts. As I loaded the young men I felt their agony and terror, and I also felt unbelievably sorry for them. I knew, and they knew, what they were facing.

We took off from Long Binh in a convoy for Saigon, with MP Gun Jeeps in front of us and behind us, and made our way into the city, where within an hour we arrived at the hospital / torture center. We took out the prisoners and handed them over to the Vietnamese guards, then reconstituted the convoy to make it back out to Long Binh. Upon leaving the place I noticed that the front entrance to the hospital was decorated, weirdly, with these happy-like, Disneyesque, plant sculptures; Mickey Mouse, Donald Duck, and the rest.

The empty convoy headed north along Highway One, back to Long Binh. An MP Gun Jeep led the way. I was driving the second ambulance behind the Jeep. We were doing our max of about fifty mph when suddenly the driver of the gun Jeep, for no apparent reason, slammed on his brakes causing a chain reaction convoy accident. I saw him hit his brakes and watched the ambulance in front of me hit his brakes as well. I was able to stop without hitting him, but from behind me came another ambulance barreling right into my rear with exploding force. The ambulances to the rear also piled into each other. The pileup destroyed several vehicles, all because of the idiotic behavior of the MP driver in the leading Gun Jeep.

When I returned to the 584th, Sergeant Adams met me. He'd already heard about the accident and was determined for whatever reason to pin the blame on me. In front of other guys, he gave me a degrading chewing out for causing everything. I knew that wasn't the case, so I went back to the hooch trying not to let this little jerk get to me. The next day, Adams came up to me and apologized personally, but not in front of others. He had read the official MP report on the incident and realized that it hadn't been my fault.

What tormented me about the POW convoy mission was the knowledge that the young men we delivered would be lucky to make it out alive from the place we had delivered them. They were boys, maybe eighteen years old. One of them, in a full body cast, had puked in a space between the stretcher he was lying on and the inside wall of the ambulance. He'd tried to hide it from me in fear of what I might have done to him for messing up my ambulance. The puke comprised only a few kernels of rice covered in mucous.

| | |

On another morning, while waiting half asleep in my ambulance, I was ordered to go to the 93rd's blood bank to pick up some blood. I had done this often. It was a routine duty of mine. I would drive over to the blood bank, pick up a Styrofoam container filled with dry ice and many pints of blood and return it to the 93rd, backing the ambulance up into its usual space up against the ER ramp. Normally I'd then carry the blood into the ER and hand it over to the staff.

That morning I wasn't aware of any urgency regarding the blood. There had never been any urgency before. I don't know what had happened. I think I was just worn out and disoriented by everything that morning and passed out at the wheel after returning from the blood bank.

Suddenly a nurse was frantically screaming, "Where's the blood? Where's the blood?"

I was jolted awake and immediately got up and handed the ice chest to the medic with her. They took off running with it. I sat there wondering what in the fuck had happened. It was about fifteen minutes later, when I was ordered into the hospital. A stern-looking older medic, a lifer, guided me into a surgery room. As I entered the room, the first thing I noticed was that red blood was splattered everywhere. There was a corpse lying on an operating table draped with blood-soaked sheets. Standing about the body were Army surgeons, nurses, and operating room techs, all staring at me. I was the center of their attention.

The head surgeon, an Army Major, with his green surgical face mask dangling from his ears, then tore into me. He told me they'd been battling to save this young soldier who'd suffered massive injuries and was bleeding to death. They'd waited for the blood that never came. He blamed me for killing him and told me I would have to live with this on my conscience for the rest of my life. I was the guilty one. Then he shouted something insulting and profane and ordered me to get out. I left.

I recall thinking as I walked away,

No. It's this useless war that is to blame. It's the war machine and all those who believe in and support it, which many of them did, that are responsible for his death. They're just trying to escape their own guilt by pinning it on me because I am the lowest man on the fucking totem-pole.

They were suffering from "Survivor's Guilt" and trying to pass it on to me. Fuck them.

These stories I've been recounting are unthinkable in a normal world, but Vietnam was not a normal world. For me, they were commonplace experiences. Days of insanity, filled with stories like this, went on and on without end in sight.

May 31, 1969

Dear Mom and Dad.....
How are you? Things here are pretty good – it's been a pretty busy week. I don't know if I told you in my last letter that they switched me to another platoon. It seems as though there was a guy in the 1st platoon who wasn't getting along with his sergeant too well and wanted to switch, so they picked me.

It really burnt me up because I was just getting to know the guys in the 2nd platoon where I was. The excuse that they gave was that I was a "good man" and that they had a lot of goof-offs in the 1st platoon and that they figured I could help improve the situation. It beats the hell out of me why they told me that, because I'm nothing "spectacular"–I just have done my job and stayed out of trouble.

They probably had an ulterior motive though. You see – the company is recently loaded with negroes – the Commanding Officer is now Black, the First Sergeant is now Black, etc. etc. etc., and the 2nd platoon had only Black soldier. So, they switched me for a spade and got a colored platoon sergeant at the same time. They want total integration I think.

So, I went and bitched to the new First Sergeant about it and he told me that I should consider it a compliment. So, I told him not to compliment me like that anymore. I packed up my stuff and moved. And that's not half the story.

The company maintains men and ambulances at different locations, some as far away as 20 miles from Long Binh. The platoon that I was in, the 2nd Platoon, has two of them, one of which I manned for 3 months out at the depot, and another one at a place called the "Newport Docks", close to Saigon.

The 1st platoon has ambulance commitments at a place called "Phu Loi" – about 20 miles to the west of Long Binh, and another one at a place called "Bearcat", which lies about 10 miles to the east. Well, it just so happened that one of the 584th's men at Bearcat wasn't getting along with the unit that he was loaned to out there – so, my platoon sergeant decides to send me out to replace him. By that time I couldn't give a damn where they sent me. So that's where I am now – "Bearcat".

But I may learn to like it here because things are a lot less military – I think, than in Long Binh. I haven't started working yet because I just got here yesterday and today is Memorial Day (happy Memorial Day!) I guess my duties will be to take patients every other day into Long Binh. And the days that I don't do that I will be working in the dispensary giving shots, stitches, etc. It should be a good break from the monotonous harassment at Long Binh.

Bearcat is kind of different. It's mainly made up of Thailand soldiers - - a whole division of them (13,000). Besides the Thais I guess that there are a few thousand US troops here. Most of the US personal are with helicopter units – there's a lot of them here.

I was really getting tired of Long Binh. It's probably the ugliest place in Vietnam. It's really pretty here. I don't know how long I will stay before going in – I may stay here until the first week of August when I hope to go to Australia for a week. I put in for it the other day but won't know if my request has been accepted or not for a few weeks.

.........Well, it seems hard to believe but I've been in Vietnam for 6 months now.....

.........It was good to get your letter this week. I sure would have liked to have been home for our family get-together. Knowing that there is somebody somewhere who cares about you and who you care about also means a lot.

Take good care of yourselves Mom &Dad

Love, Jim

Waiting and Watching

*One of my buddies took a polaroid photo of me
sitting behind the wheel of my ambulance at
Long Binh, where I was stationed in 1969.*

Receiving casualties from helicopter

24th Evacuation Hospital, Long Binh

*Captured Viet Cong Prisoners
being led off by American soldiers.*

CHAPTER TWENTY-FOUR

Bearcat

ON MEMORIAL DAY of 1969 I had completed six months of my Vietnam tour and they'd promoted me to Specialist 4th Class (Spec4). It was then when my company transferred me to a base called "Bearcat". A much more dangerous place, often regarded by the men of the 584th as the place you didn't want to be assigned. The word was out that the enemy had recently overrun the base, killing many of our men, and that it could easily happen again. Platoon Sergeant Lank led the way in his jeep as I drove my ambulance behind him, out the dozen miles or so to the base where I checked into my new unit, the 50th Medical Company. He then left and drove back to Long Binh.

The US Army's Ninth Infantry Division had built "Bearcat" as their basecamp earlier in the war but had moved out a year before I was assigned there. They turned most of it over to the Thais; the "Royal Thai (Royal Panther) Division," a military division from the South-east Asian nation of Thailand. The US had invited Thailand, Australia, Korea, Taiwan, and other nations to send in military divisions and units to assist them in their war anti-communist effort in Vietnam. These were the so-called "Democratic Freedom

Forces." In reality they were more like mercenary armies; some of them run by criminal warlords. Of course, all of the costs for these "Democratic Freedom Forces" were taken care of by the United States.

There remained a few thousand US troops stationed at Bearcat, mostly Army helicopter and artillery units. The 50th Medical Company was a small "MASH" (Mobile Army Surgical Hospital) unit stationed there to take care of the medical needs of the remaining American troops. Commanded by a Captain who was an MD, it was a self-contained medical company with its own surgery, pharmacy, and x-ray capabilities, and a staff of about thirty medics and other personnel. I was sent there by my company to join up with another 584th medic to provide ground ambulance transportation for this unit, and it was there I would spend the next eight months of my Vietnam War tour.

I recall my first night at Bearcat. What a scary place. It was a strange and foreboding kind of scene where I knew no-one. A Black sergeant led me out to a flimsy-looking, two-story wooden shack of a barracks and said, "Gibson... fine you'sef a cot, and settle in." That night, I was invited to a private party to meet some of the guys. They were hanging around in a dark room in the flimsy shack, wearingG.I.shorts, smoking, sipping on beers, and joking around. More than half of them were Black, and I remember I got a very welcoming feeling from them. I felt more accepted and more at home with them that night than at any other time since I'd been in Vietnam. I was glad to be out there with these guys and away from Long Binh. After the get-together, I went back to my cot and laid down.

It was then that the reality of where I was sunk in. I was on the other side of the world in a flimsy wooden shack. The night temperature was a sweltering ninety degrees or more, and the humidity was something similar. Mosquitoes were buzzing everywhere, and huge bugs crawled all over me from time to time while I laid listening in the dark to the *whomps* and the *whams* of the outgoing and incoming. It came echoing in and out from all directions and distances. The night was alive with the sounds of death. It was nearly impossible to sleep.

Bob was the other guy from the 584th stationed at Bearcat with his ambulance. We had two ambulances. He drove one, and I drove the other. He was a nice guy from somewhere in Wisconsin, and I liked him from the start. Our primary job was to transport those in need of more medical care than was available at the 50th MASH, into the larger field hospitals in Long Binh. We alternated this duty. One day he was on, the next day was my turn. Our ambulances were old post-Korean War relics; each probably at least fifteen years old. They were mid-fifties vintage Dodge Power Wagons that could hardly exceed fifty miles an hour. Basically, they were large, heavy, Army green, metal boxes, painted with red and white medic's crosses on each side. These worn out, rattling buckets of nuts and bolts, with almost no brakes, often broke down and made perfect targets for the VC.

The road from Bearcat to Long Binh, though only a physical distance of about a dozen miles, seemed much longer. It was a one lane road, bouncy, sparsely paved and in some areas not paved at all. Mostly a route of ruts and potholes, it wound through jungles, villages, farms and rice paddies. It was an unsafe drive where anything could happen. The villages were rife with Viet Cong. Every other day I would gather my patients up in the morning, into my ambulance, and head for Long Binh. I would select the least injured or most capable soldier I had and sit him shot-gun, hand him my locked and loaded M16 and explain to him,

"I'll be driving this ambulance as fast as I can to get us into Long Binh. You keep this rifle aimed out the window and shoot like hell in case we should get fired on."

Then I'd take off and drive through the muddy roads of Bearcat that led to the main gate.

The heavily armed Thai guards standing duty there, seeing my ambulance approach, would quickly open the gates and let us pass. I would press the pedal to the metal and haul ass as fast as my old rig would allow. It was a ride-and-roll, bucking bronco ride the entire way. As I negotiated every rut, bump, and turn of the road, the injured and sick had to ride and endure this journey in the back as I attempted to get us through to safety. It was a hairy-scary rush of adrenaline the whole way. I was always thankful when I made it through to Long Binh, and back to Bearcat the same day. There were continuous VC ambushes that took place on this road, and I was always aware of the possibility. As days and weeks of these journeys went by I became gradually accustomed to these trips.

Bearcat was closer to the war than Long Binh. At night, we would hang together outside to watch and listen to the war going on around us. There was nothing else to do. We could see the flares being sent up from our perimeter, just a hundred yards away, and we'd hear the machine gun fire opening up. Charlie was continuously probing the line. One late afternoon, not long after they had assigned me there, our First Sergeant called us in to let us know about something. Intelligence had information showing that the NVA would be massing and moving large numbers of troops through our area; perhaps 12,000 enemy troops would pass by in the jungle, just beyond the tree line of our base defenses. We were told that if the enemy wanted to come into Bearcat, he might easily just come in.

We were on alert. Darkness fell, as we waited for something to happen. The building I was in made no sense. I think the Army corps of engineers had built the structure when nobody expected the war to escalate to its current level. Nobody had planned on this. So, there I was, trying to bunk down for the night on the second floor of a flimsy wooden shack that could easily be blown away by enemy fire. None of us slept that night. There was a sandbagged bunker, filled with muck, mud, mosquitos and rats, that was dug into the ground just under the shack we were to take cover in, in case of attack. It was around 2 am. I was half awake with my fatigues and boots on when they first came in; loud, earthshaking, *whoomphs*! Incoming rockets! Many of them coming in rapidly, getting closer and closer. I immediately got up from my cot and ran for the outside stairway, diving headfirst off the second story, landing chest first with a great thud, on top of someone who collapsed underneath me. After hitting the ground, I scrambled and crawled into the bunker for safety. When we were fairly sure the missile attack was over, we came out of the bunker and assembled in the dispensary. It was then I learned what I had done. I had landed on the back of one of our guys with my chest and squashed him right into the ground. I really felt awful I'd done that to him.

It was later that night when the title of "Superman" was given to me, in front of the entire Company, by the First Sergeant. Everyone got quite a good laugh out of it. A reputation was established for me as the "flying by the seat of my pants" kind of guy. I had literally flown right off the stairway landing and come crashing to the ground. Nobody held it against me, including the guy I'd hurt who we had to evacuate down to Long Binh for treatment the next day. His back was injured but he was on duty with us again within a week and was the only casualty we suffered that night, thanks to me.

While I preferred being out at Bearcat, there were some things about the place that were weird and scary. It was another world. One day I was driving my ambulance down a dirt road within the base when I thought I'd run over a firehose. I stopped. It was a huge, beheaded Boa Constrictor, about a foot wide and 16 feet long, lying there. Another time some guys in our unit were driving along the same road and saw a man lying there. He was a Thai soldier who had fallen off a troop truck. Apparently, the truck behind him had run over his head popping his eyeballs out of their sockets and left him for dead. We treated him at the 50th, got his eyeballs put back into his head and sent him back to his unit. One night some Thais were off duty, partying in a "Club" (whore house) drinking a lot of "Mekong" (Thai Whiskey). They got into some kind of a macho contest and played a game of Hot Potato. The hot potato in this case was a live grenade, out of which they'd pulled the detonating plug. As they passed it around to one another in their drunken state, to see who had the guts to continue on, the result was predictable. They were all blown away. I wasn't there for the pickup job but I heard there were blood and guts everywhere.

At night in the background, there was the continuous sound and sight of the war; the pounding away of our artillery batteries opening fire, and then Charlie's incoming missiles in response. We had nothing to do but hang out at night and watch the light show go on. Almost everybody got stoned and zoned out of their minds on Marijuana, especially at night. I smoked some, but not much.

June 6 1969

Dear Mom and Pop......
Howdy there! I got your letter and pictures today and sure did appreciate them. Thanks......
About this situation over here; I want you to know that I think it is wrong. We shouldn't be here and if I had my way I'd load every G.I. up and send him home as soon as I could.....
I'd also like you to know my opinions about the anti-war protesters back home and all the trouble. I think that they are right. And I respect them. But it's wrong when they turn to violence, because by doing this they are starting up something that looks just like what they are against.
Americans should be responsible enough to be able to see those individuals who are pulling off underhanded operations and grabbing power for their own sake. (whether these people appear to be student protesters or Government/Military leaders makes no difference) And when they do see and recognize who the real criminals are they should put a stop to them. But unfortunately not enough are able to tell the one from the other. It's time for the Americans to wake up – and they must do it themselves or it is no good.
There should be a turnover in the way that many Americans are making their living. There are too many Autonetics workers [war industry workers], If you know what I mean.
I wanted you to know my thoughts and how I feel because you are my family.

All my love,
Jim

CHAPTER TWENTY-FIVE

Bearcat Stories

IN MY LETTERS home to Mom and Dad, I tried to sound fine, but I wasn't. All the while in Vietnam, I struggled with major depression, living day to day, trying to just get through it. Everything about my existence there went against the grain of who and what I was. My depression was only relieved by knowing that one day my tour would end; one day I would return to "The World." I kept a calendar hanging near my cot and would cross off each day as it ended. It seemed like the days would just not end. I would check and recheck my calendar to see if I'd made some mistake. My depression grew as the days, weeks, and months went by out there at Bearcat with one horrible experience after another.

One day the radio came on notifying us that there had been an air crash out at the airstrip. Bob and I responded with our ambulances, each with a crew of medics to attend to the injured. It was a terrible scene; an Army two-seater Bronco airplane had gone down. The pilot was dead, but the other guy was still barely hanging on with grave injuries. We knew we had to evacuate him fast to Long Binh, so a helicopter pilot standing nearby ran over to his Huey (helicopter) which was sitting about a hundred yards from where we were. He took off and whirled it right down next to us and the downed plane. As he did, a ferocious wind from his blades worked up and sand blasted us all with the dried clay which was the ground surface of the airstrip. I was almost blinded. We got the surviving guy out of the aircraft, loaded him into the Huey, which then took off with two of our medics attempting to keep him going until they reached Long Binh. It didn't work. He died along the way.

After the helicopter left I saw a group of soldiers surrounding something that looked like it might be bad. There was some commotion going on and I thought there might be another wounded guy. A group of soldiers had pinned a G.I. to the ground. He'd gone berserk just at the sight of the plane injuries. The sight of it all was just to much for him. We grabbed the guy, tied him up, sandwiched him between two litters, shot him up with drugs, and transported him back to the 50th.

War breaks men down, not just physically, but mentally as well, and there were a lot of soldiers in Vietnam who suffered serious mental illness; this while the US Army Medical Corps did little to help them. Suicides and drug overdoses were common. Army brass didn't want it to get out, but these war injuries were epidemic and not being dealt with openly and honestly. The Vietnam War was a war of genocide, and a crime against humanity; it was bound to injure the souls of many of America's young men. The system wanted this all to be quietly swept under the rug.

I remember this guy in the 50th. John was his name, a pharmacist's technician, a Spec4 in grade like me. He seemed like an intelligent, conservative straight-laced kind of soldier, but that's about all that I knew or thought about him. One day I was surprised when he approached me in the barracks where nobody else could hear. He told me he trusted me to hear what he had to say in confidence. John then explained to me that there were agents among us who knew "everything" about us, who were reporting all they knew upward to superiors. He said that it was a dangerous situation for all who were stationed out there. He named a few guys within the unit he suspected as being the agents or spies. His tone and demeanor were nervous, to the point of being shaky. He was terrified and seemed kind of weird. I thought he was paranoid as hell.

Within a few days, one of my friends told me John had also approached him in similar way. Another friend reported the same thing. There were a few of us who worried about John's sanity, so we tried to help him by going to the Company Commander, the Doc, to tell him about it. Doc didn't seem to be concerned at all about whatever was bugging John and told us not to pay it any concern either. We were to forget about it.

I thought no more about John until a few weeks later, when a story came down the line that John had gone on an R&R (Rest and Recreation leave) and had never returned. They had reported him as AWOL (Absent With-Out Leave). This really piqued my interest, because John was not at all the soldier you would ever expect of this. Then, a bizarre story unfolded that John had been found walking around, nude, on a street in downtown Saigon and been brought into an Army Hospital Psychiatric unit where they'd evaluated him then evacuated him out of Vietnam for mental reasons. I suspected maybe John was not as nuts as I had previously thought he was. Maybe what he said was true and that "They" had gotten rid of him once they discovered he knew something. Was I now the paranoid one?

I did a little fact checking. On one of my runs down into Long Binh a few days later, I paid a visit to a buddy of mine, Nick, who worked as a psychiatric technician at the 93rd EVAC's psychiatric unit there. The US Military in Vietnam had only two such units, and they were the only psychiatric evaluation/evacuation units in Vietnam. There was the one at Long Binh and another one at a base somewhere way up country. If John had been taken in and evacuated from Vietnam because of mental reasons, he would have had to pass through Nick's unit for evaluation. Nick went through all of their records and also the records of the unit up north, and there was no record of John. He wasn't evacuated from Vietnam as a mental patient. So, what happened to him? That was the last we heard of John. Had he been on to something? Had he heard too much? What did John know?

105 MM Howitzer
We had several batteries of artillery at Bearcat

CHAPTER TWENTY-SIX

Operation Speedy Express

AT NIGHT THE guys of the 50th would come out and start smoking pot. I'd come out and hang with them and we would watch the nightly spectacle of war going on around us. From time to time, there would be visits from a few of the guys who were with the assault helicopter squadron just across a mud road that separated our units. There was one guy who stood out from the others; he strode by with a loaded .38 hanging from his belt as if he were some kind of cocky cowboy gunslinger from the old west. He was feared because somebody said he had killed over five hundred Vietnamese from his position as a door gunner on one of their crews. Nobody seemed to be openly bothered by this but I wondered how he could ever live with himself after committing such atrocities. I started wondering if there was something going on that we didn't know about.

A few days later I was standing in line at the mess hall one morning when I overheard a disturbing conversation. There were two "Soul Brothers" standing in front of me in the chow line waiting for their scrambled eggs. The mess-hall was dark and uncrowded, and they weren't aware I was there. It was then one of them turned to the other and said,

"Bro! I cannot believe what I saw yes-ta-day! It was really BAD man! Dig dis! Cap'n Jeffrey, he drop down into da Ville and land. Den he go out and grab a Vietnamese baby and take it out to a field! Den he get back in and go up and circle round it. Dat's when dey open up on it! Motha Fuck'a! Jus' usin' it fo' taw-get practice! It was so BAD man! Dey jus shoot da shit out'a dat litta fucka. COLD Man!"

When I heard this, I immediately interrupted and asked them to tell me about it. They hadn't realized I was there and were shocked and scared I might have heard everything. They then denied the conversation had taken place and said,

"We was jus' jive'n, Bro. Don't mean nothin'."

They denied they'd said anything. I could tell they would reveal nothing to anybody outside their unit. It was all done in absolute secrecy. Even us, the medics who lived just across the road from their barracks, knew nothing about any of what was going on. I had felt the vibes when I first arrived at Bearcat. It was a feeling of pervasive evil. My senses, my intuition, my instinct, were all overloaded, and spoke to me. This conversation began to validate my feelings. Something was going on here.

Apparently, his unit was involved with something few outsiders knew about. There was an operation going on, something called Operation Speedy Express. I knew nothing about it until its existence was reported many years later, after I had come home from the war. From December 1968 through May 1969, this large-scale operation was carried out by the 9th Infantry Division, with support from other Divisions ranging from helicopter gunships (many from Bearcat) to B-52 bombers. After it's completion officials claimed an enemy body count of many thousands at the cost of only a few hundred American lives. The numbers were just made-up to justify what was mostly a slaughter of the innocent.

Operation Speedy Express was a US Army operation of inhumane slaughter done on a massive scale, something the Army High Command in Vietnam ordered and conducted without regard to any humane or "internationally accepted legal rules of war." It killed off the old folks, women, and children living down there, not far away from where I was in the Mekong Delta area. They killed thousands of innocent people in a planned, calculated, and indiscriminate fashion, and murdered them in the most brutal ways. It was a hideous war crime kept hidden. There were many 9th Infantry sniper units operating in the daytime, but they did most of the slaughter by assault helicopters flying day and night into villages and just destroying them, opening up machine guns on the civilians. Their orders were to kill anything that moved. It was often cold-blooded murder.

CHAPTER TWENTY-SEVEN

Was it Morphine or Heroin?

I WAS LIVING in psychological hell. The only thing I knew for sure was that I had to somehow hold on, mentally and physically, until I could get out of Vietnam, out of the war, and out of the Army. I had to somehow make it back home alive. I was only concerned with getting to my "DEROS" date. That was all I was concerned with.

Marijuana was everywhere in Vietnam, and guys were smoking it all the time. You could hardly get away from it. Even though I'd been a hippie and smoked lots of pot at home before being drafted, I didn't want to smoke it while there. I probably smoked pot about four times my entire tour. Marijuana always had an intensifying sensory and emotional effect on me. I wanted just the opposite of that. I recall one night being really stoned when a bunch of VC mortars came in and how it freaked me out. I wanted nothing to do with marijuana over there. I didn't want to drink alcohol either. First, because I never had been a "Juicer," but mostly because

I always wanted to be at my absolute optimum clarity. And I did my best to stay in the best physical shape I could. During off hours I would strip down to a pair of cutoff fatigue pants and go running for miles around the base along Bearcat's berm, sometimes in temperatures approaching 120 degrees. I was serious about maintaining myself and surviving.

One night, one of my buddies, who'd been acting very mellow, said he wanted to tell me about something he'd been smoking other than pot that really made him feel relaxed and good and he wanted to know if I might be interested in experiencing this. I asked him what it was, and he said *morphine*. It was a pure, white granulated powder. He would fashion a one-inch pipe-sized bowl out of aluminum foil, hold it by a surgical clamp, then sprinkle into the bowl just a few speckles of the white stuff. Then out came a zippo lighter to heat the bowl from underneath. The powder would heat, first becoming red hot, then turn into a white smoke which he would then, through a straw, inhale deeply down into his lungs. I've realized since those days that what he was smoking was not morphine but actually an extraordinarily strong and pure white heroin, known as "China White." He would pay about thirty dollars for a 35-millimeter film canister of the stuff that at home on the street would probably go for about a grand. It was unbelievably strong, cheap, and readily available. The drug connection came through a guy from the assault helicopter squadron across the alley. He was a true junkie who would show up and start dealing, then hang around for a while to shoot up. He would inject the heroin directly into his veins like all real junkies do. None of the guys I lived with did that. They just smoked it, and that was enough.

Not long after I returned home from the war, I put two and two together, and surmised what the source of the heroin probably was. It was most likely brought into Bearcat by the Thai Generals in charge of the base. A great deal of the world's production of opium and heroin at the time was coming from an area then known as the "Golden Triangle." This was in the northern jungles of Thailand, Burma, and Laos, and it was controlled by war lords there. The Thai Generals would fly the heroin in on their airplanes and land them right there on Bearcat's dirt airstrip unchecked. From there they would spread the drug all over the country and make millions off of addicted US troops. To this day I have no proof of this, but it seems to make sense.

July 3, 1969

Dear Mother and Father.....
Another week has passed in a typical uneventful fashion and so I am left trying to assemble some interesting tidbits of information to relate to you! .... There is a happy note here. The level of hostilities has dropped somewhat during the past week and it just may turn out to be a move by the commies to show the US that they are interested in troop withdrawals. I hope so and am keeping my fingers crossed. Here's some pictures that I took today with a friend's Polaroid camera here at Bearcat.

All My Love, Jim

III

I adjusted to my situation. My life was simple: driving an ambulance full of patients into the hospitals at Long Binh from Bearcat and back again every other day. I'd make the trip three or four times a week. It was dangerous, but that was just a reality we all lived with out there. On my off days, they required me to go into the dispensary's medical clinic and work. I mostly worked in the shots and inoculations room where it was my duty to administer whatever shots were called for. I'd say that about half the injections I gave were inoculations for things like Plaque, Cholera, and Smallpox, and the other half were shots for sexually transmitted diseases, like gonorrhea and syphilis. It was staggering how much of that we saw. The whores were everywhere.

Back at Long Binh, my company, the 584th Ambulance Company, enjoyed a particular distinction as the company able to smuggle the most prostitutes into the base. The pimps would go into the adjoining towns and villages, pick up the girls, hide them in the backs of their ambulances, and drive them back into Long Binh. Everybody got paid off in the operation, gate guards and all. Out at Bearcat, it was the same. We had one "Brother" pimp named Jake who had a particular knack for this and would go out to the local villages to find and bring back the whores. In the shot room of the clinic I worked, I tacked up a Playboy centerfold pin-up of a beautiful nude babe. Before I told them to bend over so I could shoot their butts full of millions of units of penicillin, I'd ask the soldiers to turn around and stare at the pin-up and ask themselves whether it was worth it. The amount of penicillin I injected was unbelievable!

What a different world I was living in. I'd come all the way from a nice respectable, white, middle class, Orange County California town, where life was always safe and easy, and then into this horrible world of criminal war, drugs, and prostitution.

CHAPTER TWENTY-EIGHT

The Chaplain

THE DAYS WENT on and on as I melted down psychologically. I couldn't believe how long each day took to end. Once I sought the base "Chaplain" for some counseling help. He asked me what my problem was, and I told him I thought our country was committing war crimes right there in and around Bearcat, and that all of this was more than I could stand.

Nearly a year before, back at Fort Sam Houston, at the beginning of my Combat Medic's School, our training company was marched into a large auditorium where we'd been ordered to sit at attention and listen to Fort Sam Houston's base Chaplain, an Army Colonel who gave us a religious sermon. The Chaplain began by explaining to us how fortunate we were to be doing not just our country's patriotic duty, but also God's and Jesus's work by agreeing to take part in the Army as medics in a war defending our nation in Vietnam. This was especially important to our nation because it amounted to nothing other than saving humanity from the evils of Communism. As he spoke, low-level disagreeable muffled moans issued from the ranks of trainee soldiers around me. Many of the medic trainees were conscientious objectors

(COs), as was I. Some declared COs, some not. They forced most of us to be there upon threat of arrest and imprisonment. We hadn't asked to be drafted.

Some had historically grounded religious pacifist backgrounds: Mennonites, Quakers, and Unitarians, but many of us were not. I was there to be trained as a medic so I could accomplish my military service without requiring me to take lives in a war I did not believe in. We believed in the sanctity of life and in the saving of lives. We did not believe in war and killing. Especially not in Vietnam. What we were being ordered to listen to and accept was insultingly preposterous and would not be accepted.

The Chaplain went on and on, and as his speech proceeded to the point when the disagreeable moans became more frequent and louder. The Drill Sergeants perked up and took notice and paced back and forth amongst the aisles displaying their Billy clubs trying to locate the moans. Tension built. The auditorium was becoming unstable and potentially out of control. Then the Chaplain/Colonel, aware of the situation, stopped his sermon and took a different tack. The Drill Sergeants backed off. The Chaplain had just preached to us why it was so wonderful we were all assembled there in the presence of the Lord to receive his blessing as we dedicated our lives to do his bidding in Vietnam. This caused an uproar, so he asked us as individual soldiers if we had questions to ask. He wanted to see if any had the guts to challenge him. He invited us to stand and do this.

A soldier rose and said,

"Sir! I am Private Jones [so and so] of the 2nd Platoon! Sir! In the Bible it states in the Ten Commandments that 'Thou shalt Not Kill'. Sir! This means what it says and therefore it rejects any religious or Godly justification for participation in any war as war is always about killing. It is against God's Commandments. What do you have to say about this?"

The answer from the Chaplain was that it wasn't as simple as that, and that those who really understood God and the Bible had determined that when doing God's work, certain sacrifices had to be made and that he was amongst those who really understood those things and what God and Jesus, the Bible and the truth were really all about was to be determined by them.

This brought the house down. Right away, a few privates shouted disrespectful things like, "Heresy" and "Hypocrisy."

The cruder and more honest of us, including myself, yelled out things like

"Fuck you, Sir!"

The Colonel just stood with his jaw hanging in utter amazement at such insubordination. Here he was, a high-ranking Army officer on his military pulpit, in front of his microphone, frozen and dumbfounded. That such low-level scum dared to insult him was more than he could take. He didn't know how to handle us, so he just motioned to the Drill Sergeants to take control of the situation. They commanded us, threateningly, to rise to attention and file out of the auditorium. Once outside, we were marched to a nearby asphalt grinder where we were ordered to be assembled in company formation, strictly at attention. This was in late August, where the temperature in the San Antonio sun was probably over 100 degrees. They then called the order out, "Push-Up Position, Hoo!"

This meant all 250 of us low-life medic trainees had to immediately drop to the blistering asphalt and remain there in rigid push-up position for our sins. We were kept in push-up position with our hands scalding into the asphalt for around thirty minutes while the Chaplain's junior officers and training Sergeants exacted their revenge, threatening and promising us that all who had acted up would be identified and surely pay the price. Some guys passed out and had to be carried away. This was our message from the US Army's Fort Sam Houston Chaplain. It was a simple message from God and Jesus.

So there I was, a year later meeting with the Bearcat base Chaplain. He was irritated I had come to him for help. He became offended that I'd told him about atrocities I suspected were going on and he told me to go back to my unit and do whatever they ordered me to do, like a good soldier. It was apparent that God and Jesus hadn't changed their minds.

CHAPTER TWENTY-NINE

Military Justice

I TOOK OFF one morning with my ambulance load of patients to deliver to the hospitals in Long Binh. Following my usual routine, I handed my locked and loaded M16 to the least injured soldier, placed him shotgun, and told him to shoot the shit out of anything that shoots at us because I would be too busy driving. After clearing the gates at Long Binh, and unloading the patients to the hospitals, I drove out to visit my old friends at the depot where I'd been stationed months before. I pulled up to my old aid-station, got out, grabbed my M16 and entered the building. Just before I entered, I did what Army soldiers are always trained to do when entering a building with a weapon. I pointed the rifle to the sky and pulled its trigger - just to be on the safe side - in case there might be a live round in the chamber. To my great surprise, it went off. Wham! Other than practically blasting out my right eardrum, I thought nothing of it and just figured the idiot patient I'd handed it to earlier had failed to clear the weapon when he handed it back to me. No big deal. Weapons went off all the time out at Bearcat.

Just then, two Long Binh MPs came snooping around the corner of the building to investigate the gunshot. I had known these guys from months before when I'd been stationed out there at the depot. They asked me what armory I'd checked the rifle out from. I said, thinking I was talking to buddies,

"Hey guys, this rifle isn't assigned to, or out of any armory. It's my personal M16 a friend of mine out at Bearcat gave to me as he was leaving Vietnam a few months ago."

They then ordered me to stand and place my hands on the hood of my ambulance. Then they turned me around and clamped handcuffs tightly around my wrists behind my back and told me I was under arrest for being in the possession of a non-registered firearm. *What-The-Fuck!?* It was strange being driven in the back of an MP jeep, in tight handcuffs that hurt like hell. into Long Binh Post's Provost Marshal's Office, as if I was some kind of criminal. I couldn't believe what was happening because for months I'd been running the road into Long Binh from Bearcat at great peril to myself when, most likely, none of these MP fuckers had ever inched out from behind the safe gates of Long Binh. I was their prisoner now, and they ordered me to get out of the jeep and enter the jail. They told me to sit on a hard wooden bench, then gave their report about me and my rifle going off to a junior-level Sergeant sitting at the desk – a shitty little son-of-bitch who berated and abused me. He then called my company, the 584th. Soon he was engaged in a serious conversation with my company's First Sergeant. I wish I could remember his name, but I can't. We just called him "Top."

Top was a Black man, and a genuine leader of men. He was an experienced, older Army Sergeant, an intimidating guy, standing 6'4", 250 pounds, solid as hell, who would stand for no shit. I'll never forget when our company fell out for reveille formation the first morning under his leadership. All four platoons, a group of about 120 men, were dressed and covered down, standing at attention, looking at him, waiting to hear from him. He began by telling us we were a "sorry lot", and that he was there to shape up the company which had been allowed to slip into a sloppily run outfit. He told us he was going to turn it around and that he could do so because he was far superior to any man there and knew how to make things right. This man told us he could out-fight, out-think, out-run any man present. He begged for any man, right there that morning to challenge him. Nobody took up his offer. He warned everyone not to think they could pull anything on him because he was too smart for that. He said he would always snoop around the company area, watching and listening to everything. I believed him, and I liked him immediately.

There I was, sitting on that hard wooden bench in Long Binh's Provost Marshal's office, with my arms painfully handcuffed behind me. After a while, Top strutted in and went straight over to the asshole desk Sergeant and had a few words with him. Because of his dominant presence, the guards took the cuffs off me immediately and soon I was leaving the jail with Top. He got behind the wheel of his jeep and I got in the shotgun seat. He then turned to me and asked, "Gibson, what in the fuck happened?"

I told him my story and he told me not to worry about a thing. We drove to the 584th, then we went into the "Orderly Room" (Company Headquarters hooch). Top told me to have a seat while he had a talk with our white Company Commander, Captain so-and-so, about my situation. While the Army is supposedly run by its officers (Captains, Majors, Colonels, Etc.), in reality, it is run by its NCOs (Non-Commissioned-Officers, its Sergeants). A First Sergeant is usually an older, very experienced soldier who has been through a few wars and knows the ropes. Most Army companies are run by these men who tell their "superiors" (officers) what to do. The officers rarely know their asses from a hole in the ground and rely on the First Sergeants for just about everything.

After a short while, they called me into the captain's office. I entered the small office and stood at rigid attention before the young captain seated behind his desk. Top stood like a giant to his left. The Captain had the Provost Marshall's report on his desk and the charges against me right in front of him. He asked me to explain myself to him, which I did.

I told him I'd been given the rifle by a friend who was processing out of Vietnam and that I kept it even though it was "illegal" because I felt more comfortable with this weapon out there on the road than with the rifles that our company supplied us with, the M14s. I explained that the M14s were bigger and bulkier and that the M16 was a much better weapon because it was shorter and had much more rapid firepower. I explained it was much easier to wield an M16 about within the confined space of the cabin of my ambulance than an M14. I think my words went right through him because I doubt he knew what I was talking about. He most likely had never considered what it would be like driving an ambulance out on the road to Bearcat and probably didn't want to even consider doing so. He turned to Top and asked his opinion about how to handle this matter. Top was great. In a militarily diplomatic way, he suggested to the captain that, in lieu of my exemplary record, and considering the dangerous mission I had been accomplishing for the company, "Specialist Gibson should be allowed to return to Bearcat without punishment, if he would use only the weapon's issued from our company's armory."

The matter was over.

CHAPTER THIRTY

Dog Tags

WE HAD A lot of down-time at Bearcat when we could forget the war, so to amuse ourselves we played basketball and volleyball. Sometimes football. We had two dogs - Hog Jaws and Greg. They were our buddies. We felt that Hog Jaws and Greg belonged to all of us. They were our Company Dogs. One day, it was discovered Greg was missing. We soon realized that a guy who'd been reassigned out of our company and been sent to a basecamp down south in the delta, had taken Greg away from us. Naturally we were upset as we considered Greg as one our own and we were determined to get him back. This was when we devised a little side mission.

One of our guys had a connection – an officer friend, who was a pilot with access to helicopters. The chopper, a small "Loach," took off and flew south with a few of our guys onboard and easily located the base and the suspected barracks. They touched down, invaded the barracks, dog-nabbed Greg and were quickly out of there. We waited on the ground back at Bearcat. Soon, the radio came alive and we heard that the Loach with our guys and Greg aboard were on their way back to us. We all ran out to greet them. When the chopper came in, it created a commotion. Dirt and dust and everything flying around as if in a storm - blinding us - just the usual helicopter stuff. The pilot had an emergency to attend to - real war stuff - and had to cut the mission short, so the guys just jumped out with Greg. We were all jumping up and down as we saw Greg jumping to the ground and start running around under the departing Loach. Hog Jaws wasn't the brightest dog in the world, but we loved him anyway. When he saw his old friend Greg there on the ground, he became so excited and agitated he just didn't know what to do with himself. He ran out and immediately got into a dog fight with Greg. I ran out to calm down Hog Jaws. It was then one of my buddies took a picture of me, shirtless with dog-tags dangling from my neck, holding on to him.

*"Hog Jaws" and me - shirtless, with dog-tags
dangling from my neck holding on to him.*

CHAPTER THIRTY-ONE

The Night Run

MY DUTIES CONTINUE as before. I would make the trip to Long Binh every other day, and on my off days I would work in the dispensary, mostly giving shots. Life was kind of boring except for an emergency that would arise now and then. One evening we had to make a night run into Long Binh to get a soldier into the 24th Evacuation Hospital for some life-threatening reason. It must have been a head wound because the 24th was where we took those. I don't recall what it was, but it was exceptional because it was almost suicidal to even think about driving the roads out there at night. We placed the soldier on a stretcher in the ambulance and I put on my twenty-five-pound flak jacket and steel pot helmet. There were four other medics who came along for the ride as guards loaded in with their M16s, grenades, and other weapons. We made it safely through to Long Binh's southern gate, and after being thoroughly searched by the MPs, were allowed in. I made it right away for the 24th Evac. I pulled up to the ER where we immediately brought the patient out and placed him on a gurney to wheel him into the ER/Pre-Op area. We pushed him through the swinging doors of the ER and delivered him to the doctors and nurses waiting there for him. Mission accomplished.

All would have been okay, except that there was pandemonium in the ER when we arrived. The ER was dimly lit and there were several gurneys with men lying on them. These soldiers were crying, writhing about, groaning, and screaming in pain. I could see what looked like white smoke rising from their bodies, and I noticed the smell of burning flesh. I asked a nurse what was going on and she told me these soldiers had been hit and sprayed with explosive rounds containing the chemical weapon "White Phosphorous" (Otherwise known as "Willy Peter") and that they were all waiting to be taken to tubs of water where they would be submerged to temporarily stop the chemical reaction. It would continue to burn until then. White Phosphorous was so awful that if you got one drop of it on your head or your arm, it would first burn through your skin, then into your muscle tissue and finally straight through to the bone. It would continue on until it had burned straight through you. There was no way to get rid of the Willy Peter other than surgery. It had to be physically scraped off of burning flesh in surgery, and the men had to suffer until we could submerge them in the tubs before they could arrange surgery for each of them.

White Phosphorous, along with Napalm, was used widely in Vietnam by the United States military. It was a weapon capable of unleashing unbelievable psychological terror. Though both sides used it in the war, the United States dropped hugely disproportionate amounts of Willy Peter upon the people of Vietnam; enemy soldiers, women, children, and old folks. At least tens of thousands of innocent civilians were horribly burned and disfigured for life by the United States during the war. My squad and I went back out to the ambulance and drove off, leaving the horror show behind us. We somehow made it back out to Bearcat later that night alive.

Aug. 18, 1969
Bearcat V.N

Dear Mom & Dad.....
It's now Monday afternoon and I have the rest of the day to myself. I just got back from Long Binh where I dropped off some patients at the hospital there ---- they all had to go see the psychiatrist!

.... Next week at this time I should be in Sydney. I can hardly wait for that.

.... It looks as though the lull of activity has stopped which comes as expected but still is a disappointment. I'm afraid that the individuals who are managing this war (on both sides) don't want to call it off. If I was a leader of one of the sides I'd pull out immediately and let the other side have it, because there isn't anything here worth fighting over --- except pride...... it isn't worth the price of the slaughter of even one person. But unfortunately I'm not running the show for either side and must be content to look forward to better days.

All my love
Jim

CHAPTER THIRTY-TWO

R&R to Sydney, Australia August 25, 1969

I WAS ON a Boeing 707 looking out the window and down on the city of Darwin, Australia, lit up with strange-looking, yellow-orange streetlamps. We landed, got out, and went into the terminal for our transfers. I was on my way to Sydney for my promised week of relief from the war. Darwin was the first leg of the journey to Sydney. The Army promised every American soldier who was sent to Vietnam during the war, a week of R&R to "Rest and Recuperate." It was meant to improve the morale of the troops who the government knew were the foundation of the war. It wouldn't— *couldn't* – go on without us. They knew they must keep us happy somehow, and a week of R&R provided a major part of this effort. We could pick from many destinations for our R&R week. I picked Sydney, Australia. I could have gone to Bangkok, Thailand, Taiwan, or several other R&R Centers in Asia, but I chose Sydney because it was a modern western city and I wanted to go to a place that would remind me of home. Sydney was my only choice for this. I just wanted to get away from the war to a place where it was safe to clear my head for the week. I was homesick and missed my country. I'd been in the Vietnam War for about ten months and was pretty well burnt out from it all when I landed in Sydney.

It was winter in Australia in late August 1969 when I checked into a hotel at a beach resort on the outskirts of Sydney known as "Bondi Beach" (Pronounced 'Bond Dye'). The R&R Center staff in Sydney highly recommended the place. It turned out to be an old musty hotel located just across the street from the beach, but since it was winter, there was absolutely nothing of interest going on, in or around the hotel or Bondi Beach. It looked dead. I was exhausted from my trip, so I checked in and went straight to my room.

I'd been fantasizing for quite some time about what a good, hot shower would feel like. I hadn't had one of those for nearly ten months, so the first thing I did was strip down and jump right in. It was unbelievable how good that felt. It was so good I must have taken about five hot showers that night. I went to sleep and slept like a baby. I got up the next morning and went down to the hotel lobby to have breakfast. I walked out of the hotel and across the street to the beach, the famous Bondi Beach. It was winter, and the weather was cold and cloudy and threatening rain. This was a real contrast for me, since I'd just come in from the heat of the tropics. There was absolutely nothing going on around there, so I went back to my room, grabbed a jacket, and came right back down again to the hotel lobby and asked them to summon a cab for me.

When I got into the cab, I asked the driver to take me to the place in Sydney where all the fun was going on. Like maybe their trendy version of Hollywood or Vegas, a place where "the action" was to be found. He drove me quite a distance across town and into a modern-looking area filled with nice high-rise hotels, trendy nightclubs and bars. It was part of downtown Sydney and close to the harbor. I got out and asked him to come back in about an hour to pick me up, then went exploring and discovered that this area seemed a lot more fun, where I would like to spend my week. When he picked me up, I again asked him to drive me back to the hotel and wait while I checked out. He drove me once again back to the trendy part of town and I checked into a hotel there.

It was in the afternoon when I walked into a bar on the main drag across from the hotel where I was staying. When I walked in, I noticed that there were no women or tables in the bar. There were only long counters where men were standing, eating, drinking, and socializing. I was hungry and thirsty, so I walked to a counter and ordered some fish & chips and a beer. Soon I was engaged in lively conversation with a well-dressed older guy who was friendly and took an interest in me, as I was a young American soldier on leave and he'd once been a young soldier himself, fighting in WWII with the allies in Europe. He said he really liked Americans.

Things were going great, and I was enjoying the camaraderie of the bar, though I thought it strange there were no women. The guy explained to me that in Australia these men-only stand-up bars were common. They were bars where men could get together and talk about men's stuff. I said, "Okay, sounds good to me." I thought nothing more about it. We were having a jolly good ol' time, talking about lots of stuff, and the guy was being generous, insisting he buy me one beer after another. He wouldn't take no for an answer. We drank on into the afternoon and I was having a good time drinking and talking to him when suddenly he stopped, and looked at me seriously, then asked me, with a heavy Australian accent,

"Have you ever sucked a man's cock?"

I was shocked and immediately pissed-off, when, I realized what a fool I'd been. He was a fag who'd been stalking me! I stood back in repulse and pointedly, angrily asked him,

"No! Have you?"

He retorted in a shameful and guilty manner,

"I've sucked a few of them."

Right then I put down my glass, grabbed my coat, and said, "Okay, that's enough, goodbye."

I walked straight out of the bar. Fuck! I was pissed at myself for being so naive, so dumb.

Fuming, I walked across the street into another tourist bar just under the hotel I was staying called the Texas Bar. It was a darkened, smoky, full-vinyl kind of bar, and I grabbed a barstool and ordered a rum and coke to cool off. I downed one drink after another, and drank until I realized I was feeling kind of sick. I made it to my room where I began heaving my guts out. I spent the entire night and the next day heaving in my room until I got it all out of me. Some fun, huh? Welcome to Australia.

I was literally on the other side of the world in a hotel room by myself. In those days, we didn't have cell phones or computers, and in Vietnam, for low-level soldiers like me, there were no phones of any kind to call home. I'd spent ten months in a war zone without talking with my family or anyone else I knew. From my hotel room in Sydney, I dialed up the hotel's operator and asked her to put me through to my parents back in the States. I heard the dial ring a few times before Dad picked up. Then Mom picked up the extension in the bedroom, and we carried on a lively conversation that must have gone on for more than an hour. I have little recollection about what we spoke, but it was just good to hear their voices. I hung up, realizing how much I missed them and my home.

I was now sober and recovered from my drinking episode, so decided to simply spend the remaining days of my leave in peace. I went out for long walks every day throughout downtown Sydney and its harbor areas. I walked by the Sydney Opera House, which, with its famous clamshell-like roof, was still under construction. I spent most of my time meandering through the city's beautiful parks and interesting neighborhoods, reflecting. The young Australian women were healthy and beautiful. At night I did nothing but get a good meal, then retire to my room to relax and watch TV. Other soldiers who spent their R&Rs in Sydney were interested in nightclubbing and whoring, but I wasn't into anything like that. I just wanted peace and respite from the war. I was so traumatized by the war that I gave serious thought to going AWOL in Australia, disappearing somewhere off the map into the outback. I decided against it. My R&R was way too brief and soon I was back on the plane and landing in Saigon, realizing that I probably faced about four and a half more months of Vietnam before my DEROS.

CHAPTER THIRTY-THREE

Long Binh Jail

BACK FROM SYDNEY, I got off the plane in civilian clothes and hitched a ride from Tan Son Nhut airbase in Saigon back up to Long Binh. I felt free, being back in Vietnam dressed in civilian clothes. For all anyone knew, I could be a foreign journalist or a CIA operative. Ten months in the war had taught me a lot. By that time, I knew how to handle myself. I decided not to check in with my company because I was sure they didn't know exactly when I would return from my R&R, and I wanted a few days of freedom to fly under the radar. I went to look up Nick and hide out with him for a few days.

Earlier in this book I mentioned I had a friend, Nick, a fellow medic and psychiatric technician. We'd trained together at Fort Sam Houston in San Antonio to become combat medics, and it was there we'd become friends. I got my orders for Vietnam, but he went on to another more advanced Army medic school to become a Psych Tech, hoping and expecting that he would never be sent to Vietnam. His plan failed, and after his additional advanced schooling was completed, the Army ordered him straight to Vietnam anyway. As fate would have it, he got stationed with the 93rd Evac's 935th Psychiatric Detachment Clinic, located right next door to my home unit there in Long Binh, the 584th. His company hooch was less than forty feet from mine.

When I'd drive in from Bearcat to Long Binh in the

mornings, I would drop my patients off at the hospitals and clinics, then wait around for several hours before the return trip to Bearcat. Sometimes I'd go visit Nick at 935th and over time developed a better friendship, not only with him but also got to know a few of his tech buddies. They were guys who had at least four-year college degrees in psychology or something like that before they entered the Army. Different from the guys I had to live with in the 584th, I could relate with them easier.

One morning Nick told me he had an assignment and asked if I'd like to go along with him because he thought I would find it an interesting experience. His job that day was to go to the infamous Long Binh Jail and interview prisoners who had claims that they were not criminals, but just crazy – mentally disabled soldiers, unfit for service. He was to talk with these prisoners, take notes, fill out forms, and report his findings back to his company's psychologists, who would then determine if the claims were valid enough to allow them to be transferred from the Long Binh Jail to the 935th's mental ward. I thought, *Yeah, I think this might be interesting.*

Long Binh Jail, or "LBJ" as they called it, was infamous for its reputation as a place of extreme brutality, a place you did not want to have to be sent. Once, the year before I arrived in Vietnam, so I was told, the prisoners, mostly Black guys, had rioted and taken control of the prison. They tied the Warden, a Light Colonel, down to his bed and beat him to death with an entrenching tool (shovel). After they'd done this, the prisoners burnt down the prison and escaped, many fleeing down Highway 1 to hideout in the slums of Saigon. After this incident the prison was rapidly rebuilt.

I realized when I arrived at the prison that morning with Nick, that there was a program of extreme cruelty going on. We were led into the jail, where the guards frisked and checked us carefully. They then took us into its interior where the prisoners were kept. It was immediately obvious there was a brutal system of abuse in place. It was a torturous concentration camp of metal Conex boxes placed right next to each other in even rows under the hot Vietnamese sun. Each Conex was a cell where about three prisoners were kept with nothing but an Army blanket and a pair of shorts. There were no bunks or toilets in these boxes. The heat inside was extreme. They were like ovens. They showed us into one of the hot boxes where we got set up for the interviews. We spent the day interviewing prisoners–mostly Black soldiers who'd come into the Conex, three or four at a time, to tell their stories. I felt sorry for them. For us to determine whether they were "Crazy" or not was an absurd task. The Army had sent them to its jail mostly because they could not or would not withstand the insanity of having to take part in the evil of the war. I'm sure some of them were "malingerers," but who could blame anyone that malingers in a scheme of human depravity and insanity that was the Vietnam War itself?

While there, I witnessed how they were treated by the guards. They required many of the prisoners to come out of their cells and take part in drill and cadence exercises that bordered on the insane for its physical and mental demands of extreme precision. The guards would shout at them, kicking them, assaulting them, and the prisoners just had to bear up under it, or they would face even worse consequences. It was torture. Nick filled out his forms for his psychologists and after eight hours in that cell we left LBJ. I was grateful to be out of there. I was really freaking out while I was there because I was, actually AWOL (Absent With Out Leave) at the time. We came back to Nick's unit, and I went straight to my company unit with the 584th and reported in. I was back at Bearcat and within my own personal prison hell once again by that evening.

|||

Oct, 6, 1969

Dear Mom and Dad...
Glad to get your letter of the 27th. How are you feeling now Dad? Is your back any better?
There's not much new here at Bearcat. In the future, I'll probably look back and think about the good times I've had here. It's like a summer camp.
But of course I could use a change...........
Vietnam is really a pretty place now because everything is green and growing. On the way into Long Binh I travel through farm country and I enjoy seeing the farm workers working in their rice paddies with their water buffalo and brahma bulls - the cow is a holy animal here, I wish that there wasn't a war going on here so that I could get a jeep and go exploring in the jungles of South East Asia........

CHAPTER THIRTY-FOUR

A Road Story

THE US ARMY would hire Vietnamese peasants and workers to come onto the bases to do just about every kind of menial work imaginable. They were mostly women, but there were also a lot of old men and children too. They would come onto the bases each day by the thousands, typically driven in by shady Vietnamese contractors who would find old trucks to transport them. These trucks were usually old broken down flatbeds or dump trucks, many pulling open trailers. Each truck would be carrying a hundred or more people, who would hang onto anything just to stay on the vehicle. They were rolling haystacks of human cargo piled on top of one another; the Vietnamese poor, trying to somehow make a few pennies to just get by and survive another day in the war. These truckloads would come onto the roads, swerving to avoid being hit by other vehicles. In Vietnam in those years, the only rule of the road was that the biggest vehicle went first, and you had to pull off and get off the road when one was headed for you because he was going to smash you to pieces and disintegrate you if you didn't. It was simple. The US Army transported a lot of its stuff on large, five ton trucks— the equivalent of the big semi-trucks back home in the States. These trucks would command the roads and come barreling through the villages in convoys as fast as they could move, and you just had to pull to the side when you saw one approaching. They gave no quarter.

One morning, an overloaded truck of Vietnamese workers found its way out onto the country road as usual. The driver hesitated with his load of a hundred or more Vietnamese aboard, then inched his vehicle out onto the road. With little warning it came; a huge US Army five-ton transport truck barreling down the road straight toward him. I'd heard right from the start of my tour in Vietnam that Vietnamese lives were not worth much to some American G.I.'s. As an ambulance driver, I'd learned the truth. I'd heard many stories of how American soldiers would just run over and kill Vietnamese on the roads if they got in their way. They would do this without even looking back, just flattening them and leaving them for dead. It was something that happened, and we knew it. Doing about sixty miles an hour, the five-ton Army truck hit the Vietnamese truck dead center in a tremendous explosion as bodies went flying.

I was told by one our Bearcat medics who responded to that scene from our unit in Bearcat, that there were several dead, but many still alive with grave injuries; writhing and screaming on the road. Women and children and old folks were lying dying from injuries impossible to treat. Our medics saw these horrors and did the best they could.

One of our medics who'd been present at the scene of the accident just went crazy one night. He was a big guy, normally a very nice guy, a well-grounded kind of guy, who we all liked a lot. We'd been sitting around, sipping beers, when for no apparent reason, he jumped up and started yelling and pounding his fist into the air. He went outside and rolled around in the mud in the dark going berserk. Several of us jumped him because we were afraid he might hurt himself or us. One of us ran into the pharmacy and came back holding a syringe full of a drug we used to administer to guys in this condition. We shot him up and he passed out. We brought him into the dispensary and tied him to a gurney where he remained until he woke up a few hours later. By this time, he was over his fit and back to normal, so we untied him and told him to go back to his bunk and sleep it off. The next day, he apologized to us and said that he couldn't explain what had come over him. He said that on the day of the accident he had also gotten the news that one of his best friends from back home had been killed in Vietnam.

CHAPTER THIRTY-FIVE

Thai Remains

BY EARLY NOVEMBER, things were quieting down in Vietnam, enemy attacks had declined, and our government had withdrawn some troops. Nevertheless, the realities of war continued and pervaded every aspect of my existence. You just never knew what was going to happen. On a quiet Sunday afternoon, I was standing outside our shower room, enjoying a smoke, expecting nothing. Our shower room was just a concrete slab floor surrounded by some crude wooden planks and a few corrugated aluminum siding sheets overhead. It was next to the side of the dispensary, and on top of the structure stood a water tank on a wooden frame that held only sun-heated water. To take a shower you would stand under a spigot, crank a simple faucet, and get hosed off. That was it. The shower room doubled as our morgue when necessary.

I was standing outside the shower that day when suddenly a helicopter approached our helipad from the west. It came in and descended completely unannounced. It was a Huey, a "Slick." (We called them Slicks when they were neither a gunship, nor a medevac, but just a general use transport helicopter) The pilot came down hard and shut down his engines. I ran out to see what the problem was. It was loaded with dead bodies. They looked like they'd been stuffed into the helicopter in a weird and haphazard way from floor to ceiling. Right away, upon hearing the noise of the incoming helicopter, men from our unit came running out to join me, and we offloaded the bodies. We gathered stretchers and carried all the dead into our shower room. It was a grotesque, nightmarish scene. Our fifteen-by-twenty-foot shower room floor was completely covered with bodies and pieces of bodies; blood and guts were everywhere. I think I counted something like twenty dead: an arm here, a leg or a head there. Gruesome shit. They were all Thais. The pilot told us the Thais had been headed out the main gate from Bearcat in a troop truck when they'd been hit by an RPG (Rifle Propelled Grenade) round which exploded while they were riding in the truck. It blew them all to pieces. We kept the bodies in our shower room for most of the afternoon until a soldier showed up in a truck from "Graves Registration," the base morgue. He got out of his truck and, in a very calm and matter-of-fact way, said, "I understand you have some Thai remains here."

We helped him load all the dead Thais and their parts into his truck and he drove off, back to the morgue, just as the sun was setting. This was just another day of my tour. Of course, the realization that these dead men had been blown to pieces just after leaving Bearcat's front gate affected me. I had to leave from that same gate the very next morning, just as I'd done for the past seven months. At that point, I had about two and a half more months to serve in Vietnam.

CHAPTER THIRTY-SIX

G.I. Resistance and Mutiny

THE ANTI-WAR MOVEMENT back home was getting enormous, as it became clear to the nation we'd lost our way in Vietnam and we needed to get out. Soldiers in Vietnam were especially tired of the war with its opportunist officers and promoters; in it for their selfish petty careers. The soldiers had had it with having to put their lives on the line for something that was, in reality, mostly about three things: American political careers, American military careers, and American corporate war profits. This war had nothing to do with defending America or Vietnam. The soldiers began to revolt.

Often this rebellion was expressed by something that came to be known as "Fragging." As my letter home to my parents explains, "Fragging" incidents even happened at my company headquarters in Long Binh :

Oct. 29, 1969

Dear Mom & Dad,
This month is almost over now. That's eleven down and three

to go. I hope that this finds you feeling well. My company in Long Binh has had some troubles over the past few nights. In total, it's a badly run company with very poor morale.

The night before last, somebody threw two grenades (Frags) at the building where all the Officers and the NCOs sleep. That really shook the place up. C.I.D. (Army Intelligence) agents were crawling around everywhere asking questions. Luckily, no one was injured in that incident.

And then, to add to the insanity, somebody else threw another one at the same building last night. That one injured two enlisted men who sleep right behind the NCOs. I haven't heard how badly they were hurt. From what I hear the C.I.D. went through the company and tore it apart looking for any other grenades that might lay around and in the process found a lot of marijuana. I really don't know what's happening there now, but I'm glad that I'm still assigned out here at Bearcat.

Love, Jim

Fragging came to be the term used to describe the deliberate attempted murder of officers in the Vietnam war by soldiers who would toss "frag" grenades into their tents and hoochs, usually during the night when the officers were sleeping. It had gone on throughout the war but it increased in activity as the war dragged on and became increasingly unpopular, especially in 1969 and through 1972.

The US Army was in disarray and collapsing from the bottom up. As I mentioned in my letter to my folks, I was glad to be away from the craziness at Long Binh, and content to serve the remainder of my tour at Bearcat. I hated the Army, its officers, and the war but was, and have always been, opposed to violence, especially murder.

|||

Nov. 11, 1969

Dear Mom & Dad,
Hi, how are you? How's life in "The World" as we say over here.

Not much happening around here.........
When I get home I think I'd like to try and do something which would be of some help to these suffering Vietnamese people. There isn't much I can do in the Army except to be kind to them when I can. You see, the Army frequently works directly against the common soul.

Also, I'd like to do something about the way we run our military machine. I'd like to see it gone – but I don't think that that would be wise. Anyway, no military would be better than the one we have now. I can't see how little me could alter the course of these things but I cannot accept them as they are – because I'd hate myself for sure then.

Do you see? Of course you do. I guess, even if when I get to be an old, old man, and I realize I haven't moved as much as a molehill during my lifetime, I will be content with the fact that I never accepted the things which hurt the world's poor pawns – the women, little children and innocent ones. At least then I will have my own mind – I will know my fallacies and myself.

With Love
Jim
80 days!

Nov.24, 1969

Dear Mom & Dad....
Howdy. How are you and what's new? The weeks are slipping by and I get a little eager to leave–I'm so tired of this.

What's happened to my mind, I don't really know. Will this make me a better person? Does war help a man? If ever I was disgusted with the world before, it doesn't compare with my feelings now. I'm a little less likely to put forth any strange or differing opinions than before all of these military experiences for fear of getting my toes stepped on. Fear of speaking up, a legitimate fear in this world of ours. Seems like a cowardly thing doesn't it? I guess it might be – all the heroes are dead anyway.

But I really shouldn't be rapping words like these to my parents. So I'll quit. I just get tired of writing about nothing, that's all.

All my love
Jim
P.S. 68 days!!

CHAPTER THIRTY-SEVEN

Back to Long Binh

IT WAS DECEMBER 14, 1969, when I was surprised by the sudden arrival of my platoon Sergeant from Long Binh. Sergeant Lank. He ordered me, with no warning or explanation at all, to gather my stuff and load it into an ambulance that he and another Sergeant had driven out from Long Binh. I was being reassigned back to Long Binh to be replaced by another soldier. I hated having to move back to Long Binh, but orders were orders and I had no choice but to comply. I came back to the 584th, after serving close to eight months at Bearcat to assume the same duties I had before I was assigned there. It was the twenty-four hours on and twenty-four hours off routine again, where I would usually drive an ambulance to the 93rd Evac early in the morning and wait until I got orders to transfer patients or other duties.

I had been back in Long Binh for no more than a few days when I learned the reason for my reassignment. I knew enough of the right people to ask. They gave me the low-down. It wasn't because of anything I had done, but because of something my replacement had done. He was the Frag bomber! CID (Criminal Investigations Command) had determined he was the guy who'd thrown the grenades into the Officer's and NCO's hooch! He'd almost killed them all. I figured they wanted revenge. They wanted him out of there, so they sent him out to Bearcat to replace me. I thought about this long and hard for days and couldn't figure out why they did this instead of just arresting him and sending him straight to the Long Binh Jail to face court marshal and eventual military execution. In retrospect, I think it may have been that they wanted to move him out to Bearcat so they could just assassinate him. I never found out, but many years after the war, I did learn from an old buddy of mine who had served with me out at Bearcat, that they sent no one out to replace me.

| | |

December 14, 1969

Dear Mom & Dad....

Hi! How are you? Sorry I haven't written in a little while – the days are going by fast. Today I was moved again. My company brought me down from Bearcat to spend some time in Long Binh, as they are very short on personnel. I'll probably stay here until I get ready to leave Vietnam. I don't want to tho – I'd rather be at Bearcat because I have some good friends there and you don't have to worry about the petty little things that you have here, such as saluting officers, etc. But I'm getting "short" anyway and I think that I can put up with it for a while.

Well Christmas is just about on us again. And this will make two of them away from home (in Vietnam). I hope that you can enjoy yourselves and don't let the fact that the family is spread over the world hide the fact that we are and always will be together no matter what happens.

Merry Christmas
All my Love
Jim

CHAPTER THIRTY-EIGHT

Deliveries

ONE MORNING I, along with another medic, was ordered to report with my ambulance to the Long Binh morgue for a special assignment. I found the morgue, pulled in, and went into the office to report. There was a guy wearing civilian clothes who was introduced to us. An officer explained to me that the civilian was an "American Advisor" who would be in charge of us and the day's mission. I was asked if I understood and I responded "Yes, Sir!" I'd been in Vietnam long enough to know that "American Advisor" was a code word for CIA Agent. This agent looked sleazy to me.

They took us back into the interior of the morgue and led us to a freezer room where coffins containing bodies were stacked ceiling high, row after row. Right away, a morgue attendant rolled out a coffin and opened its top. He zipped open a black body bag and peeled it back so we could see the object of the day's mission. Lying there with eyes closed in complete peaceful repose was an old Vietnamese man, the spitting image of Ho Chi Minh himself (see Ho Chi Minh). There was something about his face that commanded respect.

Then the CIA guy explained what the day's mission was to be all about. We were to deliver the old man to his family and his village, a village the Advisor "handled". I asked him how the old man had been killed and he told me that gunfire had hit him in a cross-fire and he was then sent to a Vietnamese hospital. His wounds had become infected with gangrene and he'd died there. I then asked him who shot him, and he said our troops had shot him but his family had been told it was the VC who'd done it. We took the old man out of the coffin and the body bag and placed him on a stretcher, loaded him into the ambulance, and took off. The CIA guy led the way in his jeep, which he drove with one hand on the wheel and the other grasping his M16 rifle.

We entered the village from a path off the road that led out to Bearcat. It was a dirt path down off the road about a mile; an idyllic, beautiful place of thatched huts, shaded and surrounded by thick stands of palms, bamboo, and tropical forest. As we drove into the village, its inhabitants came out to greet us, many of whom were wearing black pajamas. US soldiers normally associated black pajamas as being the uniform of the Viet Cong, so, to be down in this village surrounded by these people gave me the creeps.

We drove down into the center of the village and stopped. Right away a crowd of villagers surrounded my ambulance. The CIA agent immediately got out of his jeep then engaged in a long conversation, in Vietnamese, with an old woman who seemed to be the tribal leader of the village. The conversation went on for quite a while as more and more villagers surrounded us. The agent then told my partner and me to open the ambulance doors and bring out the body. As we did this, the crowd gathered closely around us and began to wail. When we laid the old man on the ground, they began screaming in horrific grief and disbelief. They became increasingly hysterical. In an intense moment, I realized beyond any doubt the man we had brought to them was truly a man of great significance to them. I have never in my life seen such mourning.

The agent signaled to us we should get the hell out of there right away, so I started up the rig and quickly drove out of the village, back up to the road to Long Binh, thankful we had not been blown away down in the Ville.

|||

It was late in the afternoon while standing by at the 93rd Evac when they called me into the hospital for another assignment. Lying on a bed in one of the ER rooms was a young Vietnamese girl, about ten years old. She'd been killed early that morning when a missile landed near her family's home, not far away, in the village of Ho Ngai. The VC were aiming for the American Air Base of Bien Hoa, nearby. Nobody told me if she was alive when they first brought her in to the 93rd that morning but judging by the wound she had I doubted it. A tiny fragment from the exploding missile had gone through the wall of her home and pierced her skull, leaving an almost unnoticeable mark on the side of her forehead. Such a tiny but fatal wound. They ordered my partner and me to deliver the girl to her family. We brought her out on a stretcher and loaded her into the ambulance and left the main gate, following an MP jeep who led the way. It took only a short time to get to her family's home, a house located across the street from the air base. It was almost dark when we brought her there and hand carried her into the main room of the house and laid her down on a bamboo bed. She was such a beautiful child. So pretty, so innocent. The family was so overcome with grief that they could not speak; too shocked to express anything. They couldn't, wouldn't believe their eyes. She was gone. We slid her off the stretcher, said we were sorry, and left.

|||

There was a little boy, a two-year-old toddler, whom I was ordered to take to an orphanage. Once again, we headed out the main gate, following an MP Jeep. The MP had an Army nurse, and another woman riding with him. I didn't drive this time but sat in the ambulance passenger seat holding the little boy while my partner drove. He was an adorable, beautiful child who hugged me along the way, causing me to fall in love with him immediately. We found the orphanage, a destitute, austere looking place, and parked the ambulance. I brought the little guy through the front door where I was met by a stern-looking Vietnamese Catholic nun in full habit. I didn't want to just let go of him, so I followed her into a room where I finally released him to her. She took the child from my arms and disappeared. He was gone.

I was left standing there in a room with fifty cribs, each holding a tiny child. I was overcome by fifty pairs of eyes staring at me, following me, each child begging me to come and pick them up; to hold them, to care for them, to love them. They were the unwanted children of the Vietnam War. The Army nurse told me the little boy I had brought in had been left at the 93rd Evac and just dumped there. She explained to me he was an "Amer-Asian" child, one of uncounted thousands just like him. His father was most likely an anonymous American GI, and because of this he wasn't wanted by the Vietnamese people.

She said this Catholic orphanage would take him in. The image of those children focusing their eyes on me stays with me to this very day.

CHAPTER THIRTY-FIVE

The Priest

ONE DAY I was on call, waiting in my ambulance outside of the 93rd Evac's ER, when I noticed a Catholic Priest trying to change his jeep's flat tire. He didn't know what he was doing so I walked over to help him. An imposing figure, he appeared as an amazing stereotype of a real Catholic Monk, wearing rough sandals, dressed in a brown woolen frock with a rope tied around his waist. He looked sort of like a noble, strong, and well-built version of "Friar Tuck" from the old *Robin Hood* series I'd seen as a kid. He was grateful for my help, and we worked together in the blistering sun for a while until we changed the tire.

I was curious, wondering what in the world a middle-aged monk like him was doing, apparently traveling around Vietnam alone in an Army jeep. I started asking questions. He told me he was a Canadian Jesuit Monk running a Catholic orphanage in the nearby city of Biên Hòa. He began by saying he and his church had tried to keep away from the politics of the war, favoring no side, and he was only doing the "work of the Lord," trying to save the children. But soon I realized what side he really was on. He was anti-communist, as were most Catholics in Vietnam.

He told me an awful story. He said that just a few weeks before, many of the children in his orphanage had been killed because of what the Viet Cong had done. The Viet Cong had staged an attack against ARVN (Army of the Republic of Vietnam) forces, close to his orphanage. Immediately, US Army helicopter gunships in support of the ARVN went up and began their counter-attack. There was vicious street fighting going on when the VC ran into the orphanage thinking the US Army would not attack them there. They were wrong. The gunships guns and missiles blew the hell out of the orphanage killing the priest's children. He blamed the VC, not the Americans. I surmised this noble-looking monk to be full of shit, because it was the US Army gunship crews that had killed "His" children, not the Viet Cong.

| | |

Dec. 21 1969

Dear Mom & Dad...

Merry Christmas! "SHORT" 41 Days! This is my childish way of saying that I'll soon be out of the Army. Thank God!

It's really hard to believe that this is Christmas and my 2nd one here............

The day after Christmas I may take an "In Country R&R" to a coastal town called Vũng Tàu which is about fifty miles to our South East. I'm the only one in my company who is authorized an "In Country R&R" because I just came back from spending more than seven months in Bearcat which is considered a field area. Long Binh is the "Rear" if there can possibly be one in Vietnam due to the absence of any real fronts. I'll only be able to spend three days there but it will be a good break from all this baloney in Long Binh. I'd rather forego the comforts of this place for the slight peace of mind I had at Bearcat......................

...........I don't want to give you the impression that I think this (War) is right. I still hold that this war is and always was senseless. America shouldn't be so stupid to allow herself to get mixed up in activities that don't really concern her. I think that the real fault lies in Europe. Britain and France and the rest really got things off to a bad start over here and somehow managed to pawn off the fight that they started on the Americans. And then they turn around and criticize the States for being war mongers. The really terrible thing about this war is that it signifies the end of American innocence in world politics. America is no longer a healthy bounding child where everything is as it should be. She has gone through her growing pains in Vietnam and is starting to grow feeble.

But this is nothing to lose hope over because it will all work out for the free man someday no matter what happens. The important thing is that we don't close our eyes to the problems we face. Meet the problems head on and if you get beaten down then lick your wounds and figure out what you did wrong and then try again. But this is all what you've been trying to teach me all my life and I know you really know what it's all about but I like you to know what I think about anyway.

Merry Christmas & Happy New Year
Love, Jim

CHAPTER FORTY

Vũng Tàu R&R

THE DAY AFTER Christmas, 1969, the First Sergeant of my company, Top, told me that because I had spent so much of my tour out in the field, I was authorized an "In-Country R&R" to go to Vũng Tàu, a resort town on the coast. It was a place soldiers all over Vietnam longed to visit. He told me to get my shit together and walk right on over to the 45th Air Ambulance Company that was part of our battalion at the 93rd Evac. He said I should hop on one of our choppers heading out for one of our units out at Vũng Tàu for a three day "In-Country R&R." Everything had been cleared, he said.

I said "great" and did just that. The Huey went up, and I rode it for the fifty miles out to our Air Base at Vũng Tàu, got off the chopper and made my way to the R&R Center to check in. The Sergeant there asked for my orders. I didn't have any. He said, "What in the fuck are you doing coming in here without orders? You need orders to come here for an R&R." I told him that my company First Sergeant hadn't provided me with official orders (Army documents) but had told me I was authorized and cleared to come out here. He said that that would not suffice. He asked what company I'd come from and in no time, he was on the land line with Top. They talked for a while as I watched the Sergeant's face turn from a negatively controlling attitude to one of complete bewilderment. He then handed the phone to me to talk with Top.

"Gibson, what in the fuck are you doing? You don't need any fuckin' orders to be there. Just head on out of that stupid shit R&R Center on you own and have you'sef' a real good time. Go downtown and enjoy you'sef. You got it?"

I said, "Yes, I think I do Top, thank you."

I handed the phone back to the R&R Sergeant, who spoke with Top for another few minutes, then hung up. He told me, "Soldier, I cannot admit you into our R&R Center. You are on your own here".

I left the R&R Center and walked out to the road leading into the town of Vũng Tàu. From that point on I was a civilian, traveling on my own, not knowing where in the fuck to go. I just stood in line with the locals for a taxi. I soon found myself, hunched down, riding in the back of a three-wheeled motorcycle Lambretta Taxi, headed downtown. The taxi was loaded with peasants, whom the driver would drop off and pick up along the way. Soon I was downtown in the harbor area where I got out of the Lambretta and wandered around, exploring. I didn't know where I was or where to stay in this foreign place. At the center of town stood a stately, run-down, old French Colonial-style hotel that looked as if it could have come straight out of a Graham Greene novel; white plaster with weather-beaten green shutters, surrounded by tropical palm trees. It must have been the town's original hotel. I checked in, then went up to my room on the third floor, settled in, and relaxed for a while. It was a large room with tall white plaster walls and a large, slow-moving fan. There were no glass windows, only open wooden shutters looking out and over what was a tropical paradise below.

After a while I put on my civilian clothes and went down to the hotel bar for a drink. There were a lot of shady-looking CIA types hanging out in the bar drinking and being hustled by the "Saigon Tea" girls. It was all very intriguing, seductive, and dangerous. The next day I went out to do a little exploring around the town. I hailed a "Pedi-cab," (a bicycle with a seat in front). This one was being pedaled by an old Vietnamese man wearing the typical conical peasant's hat and sandals. I handed him a five hundred Piaster note (Vietnamese currency that equaled about five bucks US) and said,

"Papa San, you take me all around Vũng Tàu."

He said "Okay G.I., you Numba One! I take you!"

We took off with me riding under an umbrella in the front and him peddling behind. He pedaled me around for a while in the central G.I. tourist part of town, made up mostly of bars and whorehouses that catered to the American soldiers on their R&R leaves. It reminded me a lot of the old seedy side of Tijuana; dirty, smelly, and criminal. He pedaled on.

Without warning I suddenly found myself in a different part of town. The old man had turned off the main drag, onto a dirt road, and pedaled me quickly downhill into a different part of town. He pedaled me right into what I could immediately tell was a Viet Cong neighborhood, and he did so with a broad smile on his face. There were no Americans there.

As we rode along into this neighborhood, old men and women and children came out of their multi-story tenement slum dwellings to laugh at me; the stupid American kid. I was at their mercy. They could have easily killed me or taken me prisoner if they'd wanted to. They all knew it and had a good time with what they were seeing. There I was, like an idiot, being paraded through Viet Cong territory right before them.

I said, "Papa San, let's go back to hotel, okay?"

With a big smile on his face said "Okay, G.I."

Thankfully, the VC were not into killing or capturing a dumb Army soldier that day. Afterwards I cursed myself for being so stupid as to have been caught up like that with not even a pistol to defend myself. Thankfully, I survived. I realized later that the Viet Cong owned Vũng Tàu but left it alone as they were mostly interested in profiting from the American Army's whoring, drugs, and other vices. This R&R town provided economic opportunities for them to fund their insurgency; to buy weapons, ammunition, and things they needed.

My next two days in Vũng Tàu were a great diversion from the war and Long Binh. I went out to the R&R beach where lots of G.I.'s were swimming and surfing. It was as picturesque as one could imagine a tropical paradise to be with its tall palm trees, lush gardens and deep blue ocean It was great, except the eighty-five-degree water temperature wasn't much of a relief from the horrible heat and humidity. I swam out into the surf and the South China Sea and looked to the northeast, fantasizing about swimming across the Pacific Ocean all the 12,000 miles to 15th Street in Newport Beach.

I was enjoying myself in the surf, body surfing in the waves, when suddenly out of nowhere appeared an Army Huey Cobra Helicopter Gunship. He swooped down and was only a few feet off of the water heading straight toward me when he put his nose down and aimed his mini gun at me, pretending to strafe me in the water. As they passed by, I could see the pilot and his gunner inside their cockpit laughing at what they were doing. It was just great sport to them to scare the shit out of the soldiers who'd come there to relax for a few days away from the war. They, like the Viet Cong in the neighborhood where I could have been killed the day before, were getting kicks out of fucking with my mind.

Before setting off for Vũng Tàu, I'd planned to meet up with a young Vietnamese friend of mine by the name of Tang. He was a seventeen-year-old Vietnamese kid I'd become friends with when he was assigned to ride along with me in my ambulance as part of the government's Vietnamization Program. It was in 1969 that the Nixon Administration decided to turn the conduct of the war over to the government of South Vietnam so that American forces could begin to withdraw. This involved training and equipping their military forces.

Tang told me he and his family were also going to Vũng Tàu that weekend to vacation and suggested we get together. I agreed. It would be a chance for me to meet his family, so we made plans to do so. I don't recall how we met up in Vũng Tàu, but he found me and took me on the back of his motor scooter from my hotel across town to where he, his girlfriend, and his family were staying. As we rode into that part of Vũng Tàu, I got the same creepy feeling I'd had when the old man pedaled me into that VC neighborhood a day before. I was the only American in sight and I stood out at about a foot taller than the average Vietnamese. Tang parked his scooter on a densely crowded street, and walked me up about four flights of rickety stairs into the room where his family was staying. This unbelievably shabby "hotel," for lack of a better word, was crowded with poor Vietnamese peasants who'd come by buses from Saigon to get away from the everyday drudgery of their lives for a weekend by the coast. There must have been a thousand of them staying in that dilapidated building. Many of the rooms didn't even have doors. At best there was one toilet on each floor. People were squatting about in the hallways, in torrid, humid heat, socializing, smoking, drinking, and cooking on improvised stoves. The powerful smell of *Nuc Mam* (fermented fish sauce) permeated the place. It was disorienting.

Tang introduced me to his family, but none of them spoke English and I could speak no Vietnamese, so it was awkward. There was another thing. I got the distinct feeling that my presence there was making Tang's family nervous, and I was getting vibrations that this was wasn't a safe place for me to be; not a pleasant situation for me or his family, and it was apparent I should go. So after some tea, I thanked them and asked Tang to take me back to my hotel. I politely said my goodbyes to his family and left.

I believe this experience upset Tang, as he so wanted to be friends and somehow bridge the cultural gap between us, to make things better in this horrible life that all of us were having to endure. He'd brought me to meet his family and become friends, but it really wasn't possible. He sadly rode me back to my hotel.

There I was, in late December 1969; staying in an old French hotel in the once French Colonial sea-side resort town of Vũng Tàu. I laid back on my bed in my high-ceilinged white plaster room, drinking a cold beer, reading a popular book, *The Armies of the Night* by Norman Mailer, under a large, slow-moving fan. This was an anti-Vietnam War book, that seemed like what I needed to be reading. I was hungry, so I called in the floor attendant and ordered a fish dinner to be delivered to my room, along with more cold beer. The fish dinner arrived, and at first, I was reluctant to eat it. The chef had taken an eighteen-inch fish, fried it whole in butter and oil and sautéed it, French-style, in a wonderful blend of breadcrumbs. What bothered me was that the fish's eye was staring at me as I ate it. That was disconcerting, but I ate it and it tasted wonderful. The book and the beer and the fish dinner, along with all the other strange, dangerous, and exotic, Vũng Tàu experiences, put me into what I would call another space. I was living in a very different world.

The next morning, I took a Lambretta back out to the Vũng Tàu Army Airbase and caught a flight on a small Caribou cargo plane directly to Bien Hoa Airbase. From there I hitched a ride back into Long Binh and reported back to my company, the 584th. I had only about three more weeks to go on my tour before I could get the fuck out of Vietnam and out of the Army.

|||

January 5, "70"

Dear Mom and Dad......

Hi! How are you this week? Dad, I haven't heard much out of you lately – what have you been up to?

There's nothing new here like always except that I'm getting "shorter" all the time. I hope I don't freak out like some people have been known to do during their last days over here – actually I'm not too worried about that.

There is an emotional problem commonly called "Short-Timers's Syndrome" by the doctors here. A fast change always causes high emotions in people but I really like new surroundings anyway. Boredom will kill you if you let it.

I've managed to pick up a cold this week which I think was brought on by a flu shot that I got a while back. When I get back to California I'll probably be susceptible to the flu virus – that's why I got the shot............

Well, that's about all for now. Write soon and give my love to the family.

James

CHAPTER FORTY-ONE

Last days in Vietnam

ALL SOLDIERS IN Vietnam had a DEROS date. This date was what we depended upon to give us hope for survival. As soldiers got closer to their personal DEROS, they might become preoccupied with the fact that they only had a short time left in the country. Some soldiers became flooded with fear and anxiety of any harm befalling them on their last days. This condition was known amongst soldiers in Vietnam and our Army Psychologists as "Short Timer's Syndrome." I was going through my personal Short Timer's Syndrome and found it very difficult to sleep, but I just continued to take things a day at a time and do my job. Almost every day of my Vietnam tour had a story.

|||

I've included many of the more climactic stories of my tour in this book, but there were so many other experiences. Here are a few occurrences from my last days:

One day in the late afternoon I was sitting outside the

584th's CQ (Headquarters) hooch having a smoke when the base air-raid sirens started blaring. Missiles came into the base, exploding here and there. Then there was a tremendous flash and explosion. Its shock wave was incredible, practically knocking me over. A gigantic, mushroom cloud went up right before my eyes, not more than a half mile from where I stood. The ammo dump had been hit! We all immediately ran into our combat bunkers until we were sure that the incoming attack was over, and things were not falling from the sky. One young soldier, a new arrival, went nuts and began screaming, so the rest of us grabbed him and held him until he calmed down.

| | |

I was still required to do the twenty-four-hours on and twenty-four-hours off ambulance coverage routine. What that meant was being up throughout the night and being called to some strange and stressful situations. Many of our calls after midnight were to respond to injuries at the Long Binh base bars known as "Enlisted Men's Clubs." These were shabby barns where low-rank G.I.'s would go to get fucked up, mostly on beer, then get into violent brawls with each other. It was practically a nightly ritual on Long Binh Post. One night we got a call to report to a particular EM club. When I arrived, a guy was being held with his face smashed into the ground. He was drunk, and by this time very much beaten up and pulverized by other bar brawlers. I knew I had to get him out of there, so I asked a few soldiers to help me sandwich him in between two litters, tying him in securely with straps so he couldn't break free. I got him loaded into the ambulance, lying on his back, feet forward and head to the rear. He was lying there, strapped in, staring up at the ceiling of the ambulance, when I realized I couldn't close the back doors. I just took off with him lying there restricted on his back when he began projectile vomiting upwards, spraying his vomit out the back of my ambulance like a volcano into the night as we drove along with my ambulance doors swinging freely. Realizing the situation, I laughed hysterically, not worrying that he might aspirate his vomit into his lungs and die. I was pretty nuts by this time and really couldn't give a shit.

| | |

One afternoon, our company got a call notifying us of an emergency situation, on the other side of the base requiring many of our ambulances to respond immediately. Apparently, there was a "race war" going on involving Blacks and Whites. I took off and arrived at the scene, but by the time I got there, it was all over, and other ambulance crews had already taken away the injured. An MP told me what had happened. Black soldiers and white soldiers, serving together within a logistics company started fighting with each other; it got to the point where they started shooting at each other with M79 Grenade rounds. There were a few dozen men injured as I recall, but no deaths. Racial tensions on the base were sometimes extreme.

| | |

Before they could discharge me from the Army, I had to undergo a "Reenlistment Talk" with an Army Reenlistment Advisor. This was a requirement. The advisor was supposed to explain to me what great opportunities were to be had if I volunteered and remained in the Army. I was just days away from getting out. He was an older Sergeant, a vintage World War II veteran, a good guy who I didn't know well but liked. I don't recall his name. He'd been through it all for decades and was probably one of the most senior and experienced soldiers in the entire company. It was his job to convince us younger guys to "Re-up," to sign on with the Army for another hitch. He started out the talk this way,

"Gibson, I have been looking through your record and realize it's exemplary. You have conducted yourself well and your record shows it. Not only that, but I've taken notice of you and you seem to be a good soldier. The Army would love it if you would reenlist. It is required of me to have this talk with you, and I am supposed to encourage and advise you to re-up and all of that shit. But what I want to tell you is that I would not do so if I were you."

"Of course, I will deny that I have ever said any such thing to you. I am telling you this because of what I have observed in the Army in recent years. It has fallen apart. It is not at all the Army I knew as a young man. Actually, it is a complete disgrace, and I am ashamed to be a part of it. I'm just waiting for another year to go by until I can attain my retirement, when I shall get the hell out of the Army. I would never advise my son or any father's son to be a part of this Army."

I thanked him for being so forthright and honest with me and assured him I had no intention of re-upping with the Army. I told him they had drafted me into the Army in the first place and I would not be here if I could have helped it. We winked at each other with a mutual understanding.

It wasn't long after I had my Reenlistment Talk that I had another conversation with Top, our First Sergeant. I'd always liked and respected him, and we sat down and spoke as friends. He said that he knew in just a few days I would leave his company and that he was curious what I might want to pursue after getting out of the Army. He told me he'd looked at my Army testing results and said that because of my high test scores I should seriously consider becoming a doctor. I told him it was my intention after getting home to study law and become an attorney. He just nodded his head and said,

"Whatever you shall choose, Gibson, you have whatever it takes to succeed. You just go on and do your best, and best wishes to you."

The days wound down to the last of my tour. I hadn't slept at all for the past three or four nights, worrying about everything, wondering if I was going to finally leave this horrible place and survive. The tension was something like I'd never experienced. My DEROS date was tomorrow, and my "Freedom Bird" was approaching. I hadn't told my parents the truth about when I was going to be coming home. This was because I didn't want them to organize any kind of welcoming home party for me. I wasn't proud of serving in Vietnam. I told them I would most likely be coming back around the 1st of February, more than a week after the date I expected to be home.

In the early morning of January 21, 1970, I was driven from the 584th, again in a company three-quarter ton truck, back down to the 90th Replacement Company, exactly where I'd begun my tour some 416 days earlier. I was rewinding now. I got my stuff out of the truck and thanked the driver. There I was. Many years later I learned that the 584th ambulance driver/medic who'd driven me and dropped me off at the 90th that morning took a VC bullet round through his chest not long after I left. I don't know if he survived.

I reported into the 90th with my departure orders and was told to hang around until I saw my name and serial number come up on papers that would be posted on a long wall. They told me it would most likely take about twenty-four hours until this happened, so I should just sit tight until then. There was nothing to do but wait. Waiting with me were hundreds of soldiers doing the same thing. We were all just hanging around, sweltering in the heat, waiting for our Freedom Birds to come. Some guys knew each other, but I saw no one I knew. I spent the day smoking cigarettes and thinking of all I'd been through the previous fourteen months. The experience of leaving Vietnam was very much like that of coming into Vietnam. The same sounds and smells were there, but I wasn't afraid of those things like I'd been when I first arrived. In fact, I really wasn't scared at all. I'd become used to and desensitized to everything.

The day passed, and the night passed, and the sun rose on the morning of January 22, 1970. I was sitting on the ground, waiting, when suddenly incoming missile rounds started coming in. They were being "walked in" on us and they got close. They were big missiles. This really shook the men waiting with me to get the hell out of there. We all desperately scrambled around on the ground to find some kind of hole to hide in and realized there weren't any. To think we would be annihilated on our last day in Vietnam! The 90th hadn't provided any bunkers of any kind for our defense and we were all pissed off. Fortunately, we didn't experience a direct hit, so there were no casualties.

CHAPTER FORTY-TWO

Freedom Bird

THERE IT WAS, my silver, shining Freedom Bird, standing there on the runway. It was as beautiful as everybody had said it would be. I got off the bus and ran up its stairway and into the plane, settled in and buckled up.

The doors were slammed shut, and the pilot gave it full thrust. We were soon heading up at a sharp angle into the sky and out of Viet Cong fire range. As we leveled off, a roar went up from the men on board and we celebrated the end of our tours in Vietnam. I recall thinking then that we had won the war. I thought this because it was, during my nearly fourteen months long tour, that I had witnessed a gradual lessoning of enemy attacks, and it seemed the Communists couldn't keep up the fight for much longer. When I'd arrived there, in December 1968, our forces were taking huge losses, sometimes by the hundreds each week. By the end of my tour, the number had fallen to only dozens. I recall thinking that in about ten years, Vietnam would become a thriving Asian nation somewhat like Japan became after we'd defeated them in 1945. I thought that by 1980 Vietnam would be like that, just another American capitalist success story.

I was now on a rewind trip. The plane headed northeast and within a few hours touched down at the Okinawa Air Base. I remembered when I'd landed there fourteen months earlier and watched the returning soldiers pass by me in the terminal— how they'd appeared to me then. They were a frightening sight to behold, and I wondered how I appeared to the young soldiers who were there just getting ready to fly into Vietnam to start their tours. We took off for Honolulu. That flight in January 1970 was the most precarious flight I have ever been on. The turbulence was so extreme I was sure the wings were going to be broken or sheared off. We bounced all the way over the Pacific Ocean and eventually made it down to Hawaii in one piece. We refueled and reloaded then took off for "The World," landing at Travis Air Force Base in California, where I'd begun my tour, fourteen months earlier. It was a cold early morning, just as it was when I left.

CHAPTER FORTY-THREE

Coming Home

THEY PUT US on buses and shuttled us back to the Oakland Army Terminal to process us home and out of the Army. I hadn't slept at all for five or six days but was so keyed up on natural adrenaline that it didn't matter. The processing was brutally long as they kept us waiting, standing in one long line after another for the rest of that day and night. After about twenty-four hours of this torture, at about five o'clock in the morning, they handed me my separation papers from the Army.

I was free!

They gave us travelling money to head home so I caught a cab with four other soldiers and headed over the Oakland Bay Bridge straight for the San Francisco Airport; arriving at around six in the morning as the sun was rising, in my newly tailored Army Woolen Green uniform. I wondered if I would meet up with people who would spit on me or call me a murderer or something like that. These were the stories going around amongst soldiers in Vietnam but nothing like that happened. I walked up to a counter and bought the earliest flight out for Orange County. The plane took off at about seven and in an hour we were preparing to land at Orange County Airport. As we descended, we entered a thick layer of fog. The plane continued its descent for a while and I could see that we were just about to touch down, except there was a problem - we were not on the runway. The pilot immediately gave the plane full throttle and pointed its nose up. We climbed up to get out of the situation and were quickly out of the fog and circling Orange County. We circled around for about twenty minutes as the pilot and crew tried to figure out what to do. During this time, I sat there in my newly issued Army Green uniform and thought, *What the fuck? Is this going to be how it ends? Nearly fourteen months in the hell of Vietnam and it's going to come down to this?* I looked around the plane and noticed that the other passengers were getting pretty shaken up. I was feeling okay because I'd been living next to death for so long that it meant little to me. In my uniform I tried to assure them, with strong self-assured glances, that we would all be okay and not to worry. The pilot made another pass and failed again, and we went up in the sky again. Eventually on his third try he found the runway, and we landed safely.

|||

"Wow! You're just now coming home from Vietnam? This is going to be incredible! I want to wait here and see your family's faces when they open their door to greet you!"

I told my cab driver I just wanted him to quietly drop me off and leave. I know he probably thought that was rude but I didn't care. I got out of the cab in full uniform with my suitcase in hand and walked up to Mom and Dad's front door. The cab driver, as I had asked, left. I rang the doorbell. There was no answer. I rang it again. No answer. Then a third time. The garage door was open as it always was before I'd left two years before, so I went into the garage and found the house key on its hook exactly where it'd always been kept. I let myself in and walked into the living room where I sat down on the couch. Nobody was home, so I just sat by myself in peaceful silence. I hadn't been able to experience that feeling in a long, long time. A short time later I heard the sound of a car pulling into the garage and the kitchen door opening. Dad walked into the room and stood staring at me for a moment with a look of disbelief in his eyes.

PART THREE:

VIETNAM VETERAN

CHAPTER FORTY- FOUR

Back to The World

ONCE DAD REALIZED it was me sitting there alive on his couch, I got up and walked over to him and shook his hand. We talked at length that morning in a way different than we had ever spoken with each other in the past. We spoke man to man as two veterans of war. I saw relief and happiness in his eyes, coupled with great respect as well. Later in the day he said,

"It's time for me to pick up your mom at school now, Jim, so let's get in the car and do that. She is really going to love this."

Dad drove to the school where mom worked as a first-grade teacher, parked the car and told me to walk in and surprise her. School was out for the day and Mom was in her classroom finishing her teaching duties when I suddenly opened the door and walked into the room in my full-dress Army uniform. We both cried.

Mom and Dad were overjoyed to see me and that evening they took me to my older brother's house for a welcoming celebration. After our family gathering I went to sleep in my old bedroom and slept for many hours. When I awoke, it was dark and I felt I was alone in a strange place. I hid from everybody and everything for the next two weeks before letting anyone know I was home. The guilt was all-encompassing. I had come home but not really.

The Vietnam War was an unpopular war in America in 1970. The anti-war movement had grown to huge proportions and there were regular protests against it all over the country. As my tour in Vietnam was coming to an end, the word was out that people back home were blaming the soldiers for the war and that they would spit on us and call us "Baby-Killers" in the airports as we got off the planes in our uniforms. I was never actually spit upon, but there is one upsetting experience I cannot forget.

Before I'd been drafted, I'd become close friends with a beautiful young woman of my age, Janis Crosby, who lived with her parents a few blocks away from where I lived in Anaheim with my parents. They were Canadians. She and I would spend long hours together in her parents' home in their family room late at night, sitting on rugs, talking and reciting poetry, drinking tea, and listening to the beautiful inspirational music of artists like Leonard Cohen, Donavan, and others. It was mostly the folk scene; peace and anti-war music which was so very popular during that time when we would share our common feelings of how against the Vietnam War we were. I also got to know her father whom I came to like very much; a guy who seemed to be an intelligent, caring, kind, and understanding man. He'd also opposed the war and seemed very different from my dad.

After being home from the war for a few weeks, I finally gathered the courage to go out and get in touch with The World I had left behind. I chose to walk over to Janis's house and I trustingly rang the doorbell. The door was opened by one of Janis's sisters who informed me that Janis no longer lived there and she'd become a drugged-out hippie and moved to San Francisco. Her family hadn't heard from her in a long time, and they had no idea where she lived. She may have gone back to live in Toronto, Canada, where she was born.

As I was walking away, a car pulled into the driveway. It was Janis's father. He got out of and I approached him and said,

"Hello Mr. Crosby. Do you remember me? I'm Jim."

He looked at me with discernment and said,

"Oh yeah. I remember you, Jim. I heard you went off to Vietnam, am I right?"

I said, "Yes, just got home two weeks ago."

He replied, "Great! How many kids did you kill when you were over there?"

That was my welcome home message.

|||

Soldiers in Vietnam would often describe coming home to America dreamily. Coming home was spoken of in allegory as coming back to "The World." They wanted to deny that Vietnam, the place where they were living and dying, was real; they wanted to believe that their experiences weren't of this world, but of some other place. Once they left all this Vietnam shit behind, and came back home to The World, all would be a piece of cake for them for the rest of their lives. It didn't turn out that way for many of us. After I returned, I felt I just didn't fit in anymore. Something was wrong. I was twenty-one when I arrived home from the war in Vietnam on the morning of January 22, 1970, not realizing the miserable condition I was in.

CHAPTER FORTY–FIVE

Crazy

I'D BEEN HOME for about two months when, not wanting to go on unemployment or welfare, I applied for, and was hired by, the Texaco oil refinery in nearby Wilmington, to work as a hard hat laborer— a grease monkey. The job paid well for a young guy with few employable skills, but it was dangerous. Probably a hundred of us young guys with no experience at all were hired by the company as they were rebuilding part of the refinery.

A major oil refinery is made up of several operating units that perform different functions. Each of these units is usually separated for safety's sake far away from one another with super-heated oil pipelines that connect them. One of the most central refining units in a refinery is the "Catalytic Cracking Unit." The CCU is a huge metallic structure that is the central operating unit of a refinery. It has gigantic, thick walled steel tank chambers into which it pumps massive amounts of crude oil, which is then heated to unbelievably hot temperatures. This super-heated oil then pulses out and is transferred via pipelines to the other units of a refinery. It's kind of like the pumping heart of the refinery. This CCU was worn out and had to be rebuilt. It was a gigantic structure of furnaces, tanks and pipes that extended upwards to a height of nearly two-hundred feet.

Texaco hired hundreds of us young guys, many just discharged from the military to do this dangerous work. During the brief time I worked there I heard the talk, like whispers going around amongst the workers, of deaths there on the job. The company kept all that secret from us.

At first, I was assigned to work with the refinery's internal fire department. The company told me they had placed me there because of my emergency medical training and experience in the military. This was to my liking, and I reported to the head of that department, the Fire Chief, ready to go to work. He was about a generation older than me, probably a WWII veteran. After a few weeks working there, the Fire Chief got rid of me. He and the other men working under him, who were longtime lifer Texaco employees, didn't like me. They didn't want to work with me, because they found me strange. I was too different for these older guys to relate to, and I also thought of them as stupid guys, with lug-nuts for brains. These older, almost all white, working-class men grew up and came of age during the forties and fifties, during WWII and the Korean War years. They showed me little respect as a just-returned Vietnam War veteran. I picked up on their disrespect right away. They thought of us young guys just back from the Vietnam War as losers.

Most of them were long time employees at the refinery, making very good workingmen's wages with great medical and other benefits; this was that time considered to be the golden years for the American worker. These were loyal career employees of the company and their employment with Texaco was probably the only steady job that they'd ever known. They were locked in and secure there at the refinery. All they had to do was to report to work every day; punch their timecards, not question or disagree with anything coming down from management, and then waste away the next eight hours as the pumps and engines in the refinery did all the work for them.

I really was different—very different – from them. While they thought of Texaco as something like a great big never-ending tit, from which they sucked upon for their lives, and their family's lives, I thought of the company as toxic, polluting monstrous instrument of American capitalism. I saw my employment there as that of a wage slave, and felt my job was merely a way to earn a few bucks to get by on for a while as I looked for something else. I hated the place. I felt about Texaco as I did the US Army; it was a force consuming and destroying human lives and our planet.

After I was rejected and kicked out of the fire department by the Fire Chief and his crew, I was reassigned to work with the scaffold-making crew on the CCU. Scaffold makers build the working spaces up high in construction projects. It's a skill in and of itself, These guys build the high-up scaffolding platforms that make it safe for welders, pipefitters, and other workers to do their jobs. I reported to work early in the morning. Taking the construction elevator up, I soon found myself up a few hundred feet, looking down at the massive refinery below me. Not long after introducing myself to the supervisor and crew that was working there, I was handed a twelve-foot-long metal pipe and told to walk across an eight-inch wide plank to deliver it to a previously built scaffold about ten feet away. I froze on that plank. Just shaking; wondered if dying for this corporation was worth it. That was the end of that assignment as they realized right away I was simply not capable.

The very next day they assigned me to something even more dangerous. They told me to report to another supervisor who ordered me to go into a large empty metal furnace/oil tank to work with another worker, named Mario. This supervisor had an overbearing, obnoxious personality; an enormous white guy wearing a hard hat who considered himself to be some kind of tough bully-boy. He didn't impress me at all. Apparently, Mario, the other worker, had worked for a while under this asshole supervisor, and they seemed to know each other well and have some kind of understanding. Mario was a kiss-ass suck-up. It was explained to me by the asshole supervisor that our job that day was to climb down by ladder into a huge, thick-walled metal furnace/tank that was positioned just below the gangplank where we stood. This was where we were to begin our work. We were to work in half-hour shifts, relieving each other every half hour as required by labor safety law. The job was to go down into the tank, then to climb up on a rickety wooden ladder that ascended from the bottom of the tank and went up for about twenty feet to an opening in the tank's top. This opening was a barely three-foot-wide tube. After that, the ladder went straight up for another fifty feet. When reaching the top of the ladder we would find a small pneumatic jackhammer, which we were to pick up and begin jack hammering away at the concrete (gunite) insulation lining of the pipe. The job was to knock out the old insulation so fresh insulation could be poured back and molded into the walls of this huge pipe.

This was a dimly lit and dangerous job to be performed within a tiny space. Mario was put in charge by the supervisor and once inside the tank, he told me to be the first one up the ladder to begin working. I climbed up the fifty-foot ladder to the place where a small jack hammer rested and began hammering away. After a while, I took stock of my situation. I was way up and inside of a gigantic metal tube, with little light, depending on a rickety and unstable wooden ladder to support me while I jack-hammered and drilled into the walls of the tube for my measly pay. I seriously thought about my situation. Did I really want to die for Texaco's corporate profits? I was looking at my watch, and after a half hour I climbed down the ladder and told Mario that it was now, as required, his turn to go up there to work. He looked at me and told me he wouldn't do that and that he had the authority to order me back up the ladder to continue drilling. I looked at him and informed him that that was not part of the deal and that would not happen. I told him it was now his turn. He looked at me and yelled,

"What's the matter with you, Man? You don't want to work!?"

I looked back at him with disdain and told him to get fucked. It was now his turn to get his stupid shit-ass up that ladder.

He repeated, "Hey Man! You don't want to work!?"

I responded, "FUCK YOU MAN! It's not that I don't want to work, but it is now *your* time to work!"

I faced him off and scared the shit out of this little kiss-ass, causing him to run up the ladder to get away from me and outside the tank, then run up and tell the supervisor what was going on. I sat there inside the tank for a while and realized I was screwed. The little kiss-ass would report to the asshole supervisor that I didn't want to work, and after that, my time there would be over. After about twenty minutes alone in the tank, I took the ladder up and out to confront Mario and the supervisor. They were standing there talking on the landing, about a hundred feet up from the tanks and machinery below. I approached them and immediately Mario shrank away and disappeared. I came up to the supervisor and looked at him quizzically. He looked down at me with his hard hat bearing down and growled at me in a loud, bullying, threatening tone, "What's the matter with you, Man!? You don't want to work!?"

I approached him within a few inches of his face and

screamed at him with all of my intensity, "It's not that I don't want to work, YOU ASSHOLE! IT'S JUST THAT THIS JOB IS FUCKED!"

He sensed my intensity, stumbled back and ran, leaving me alone on the gangplank. I scared the shit out of him, and he realized he was dealing with someone who was maybe out of control. He was right because I was just inches away at that point from picking him up and throwing him over the railing. That was my state of mind then. That was the end of my employment with the refinery, and I began to think that I was crazy.

After I returned home from the war, I really didn't fit in with society and didn't know what to do with myself. I was a loner. Terrible nightmares of being shot in the head plagued me. It would happen in slow motion when the bullet would enter my brain, and everything would turn brilliantly white. It was a recurring death dream.

I had Post-Traumatic Stress Disorder and didn't know it, because in those days there was no such psychological diagnosis. When we came home from the Vietnam War many veterans became known for sometimes violent, anti-social and self-destructive behavior. We were just thought of as those crazy Vietnam Veterans; losers, who were often stoned out on drugs or alcohol. We were those suicidal, dangerous guys to be avoided. There was little help available for us. In time, PTSD came to be recognized by the psychological community as a very real, legitimate mental health condition deserving of treatment. It was triggered by terrifying events — either experiencing or witnessing them. Symptoms may include flashbacks, nightmares and severe anxiety, as well as uncontrollable thoughts about the events themselves. These debilitating symptoms may continue for a long time. I had all of these symptoms. But not really understanding my condition, I just wanted to run away.

CHAPTER FORTY-SIX

Escape to Europe

BY THIS TIME, I sensed I had to change my life. Something was wrong. I was out of it. I had saved nearly all of my military combat pay from Vietnam ("Jungle Money") and held it in a savings account. While in Vietnam, I had exchanged letters with my brother Bill, who was with the US Air Force stationed in Berlin, Germany. I told Bill that if I should be able to get through Vietnam, then I would like to take a trip over there to visit him. He replied that he would look forward to that very much. After my refinery experience, I needed to get away.

My best friend Randy wanted to come along, so we went to a local travel agent and arranged our tickets. It was in the middle of May 1970 when we flew out of Los Angeles and landed at JFK in New York. From there, we took off across the Atlantic to Brussels, Belgium. We then took an over-night train into Berlin, Germany. When Randy and I arrived, exhausted from the traveling, at the West Berlin train station early in the morning, I found a phone booth and dialed Bill at the number he had given me. Soon I was talking with him. I told him we'd arrived, and he said to sit tight at the front of the station, and he would be there as soon as he could come and get us.

We found a table at an outdoor café in front of the train station. About an hour after talking with Bill, an older German waiter approached Randy and me and began to rudely shout at us to get the hell away from his café table. This pissed me off, so I stood up and angrily told him to go fuck himself. He became hostile and the scene became intense. As I was about to punch the old German out, Bill arrived at the curb with his car. He saw what was going on and jumped out just in time to intervene. We picked up our suitcases as I yelled back over my shoulder one more time for the old guy to go fuck himself. Bill could immediately see his little brother had changed.

Knowing we were coming, Bill had arranged to take a thirty-day leave of absence. Our plan was to take off in his car and tour Europe for the next thirty days and beyond, but since Randy and I had arrived two weeks earlier than planned, we had to find a place to stay. Bill found us a hotel to stay in the heart of old Berlin. It was in the center of town, on the main drag known as the *Kurfurstendamm*, one of the few original buildings left standing after the city had been almost destroyed during the WWII bombardment. We rented a large, comfortable room with two beds and a toilet just across the hall. It cost us each just $1.35 a night to stay there. This included a continental breakfast each morning served with coffee. There was an authentic Renoir painting hanging in the room. Randy and I stayed there for the next two weeks, exploring and enjoying Berlin. We would get up in the morning, have our breakfast with coffee, get stoned on the joints we'd brought along, then go down to the *Kurfurstendamm*, jump on a double-decker bus, then just go tripping, exploring the city. We visited the parks and the monuments during the day and Bill would come over in the evenings, pick us up and we would go out drinking beer and partying all night in the bars and the nightclubs that he and his Air Force buddies knew so well.

Bill had a day off, so he suggested we cross the border at the famous "Check Point Charlie" and drive into communist-controlled East Berlin to check things out and explore. Because he was with the US Air Force Security Police, he could pass through the checkpoint unchecked, wearing his military uniform in his car which bore US Air Force license plates. But civilians had to walk through the customs procedures where we and our passports were held up and heavily scrutinized and inspected by paranoid border guards and officials. This took a long time while Bill waited for us in his car on the other side. The Communist German military guards at the checkpoint who so seriously interrogated us with pistols hanging down from their belts were straight out of a Hollywood drama. Cartoonish in their old-style communist military high-hats and uniforms, they sported monocles and spectacles hanging low on the bridges of their noses.

"Ver are Your Paperze's !!!?"

"Let me Zee Your Paperze's!!!"

"Ver are Your Paperze's!!!?"

There were helmeted communist soldiers standing around with German Shepherd attack dogs on leashes, watching our every move with their AK47 assault rifles hanging from their shoulders—like we were dangerous enemies or something. All of this cracked me up. I'd just spent fourteen months of my life in a real-life war in Vietnam, and they, with their antics, didn't scare me or affect me at all. I found these fools to be quite amusing, but I was getting a little irritated by their holding us up for so long. After about an hour of this shit, they released Randy and me and let us pass through Checkpoint Charlie to enter East Berlin. We left the guard shack and looked for Bill in his old Mercedes. We spotted him, parked as planned, about a hundred yards away from us, so we started walking toward his car. It was at this point that I really started tripping.

Something took over me. I felt like I was in a movie; a 007 James Bond kind of movie; a spy thriller kind of movie. For some reason the whole situation seemed comical to me. The military-armed guards were everywhere looking at everything with their AK47's but I didn't give a shit and I wanted to start playing my role in this dramatic movie. I played a game of chicken with the Russian AK47 guys just to fuck with their minds and have some fun. Knowing they were watching us and every move we made, I began to run and hide behind the shade of the archways that stood along the sidewalk. Randy, not having a clue what was happening, just innocently followed behind me. I ran and darted suspiciously, looking both ways from one archway to the next. Like out of a spy movie. I was hoping they were watching. To me, it was a fun game. After playing this game, we finally reached Bill in his car and climbed in. Bill exploded on me with fear and anger when we got into his car.

"WHAT IN THE FUCK ARE YOU DOING?"

I'd scared the holy shit out of him as he watched the Russian guards taking their rifles off their shoulders, getting ready to aim them at us.

"WHAT IN THE FUCK ARE YOU DOING?"

He immediately started his car, and we drove away. I was laughing about it all, but Bill was really pissed, thinking I'd just about gotten us all killed. Such was the state of my mind back then. I was out of my mind, playing with them all as if they were silly toys. I could've not only gotten us killed, but also set off a major international incident at Checkpoint Charlie that day. Bill just drove on, getting us out of that situation, wondering what in the fuck was going on with me.

Passport Photo May 1970

Something was wrong and I knew I had to get away

CHAPTER FORTY-SEVEN

Traveling Free and on the Run

RANDY, BILL, AND I took off from Berlin a few days later and spent the next thirty days travelling in Bill's car throughout many of the countries of western Europe. Our plan was to travel and spend as little money as we could, often sleeping in the car or in campgrounds or fields or anyplace else along the way. We brought along sleeping bags. This was to become an incredible journey. We first travelled south from Berlin for quite a distance before pulling into Nuremburg; looking for the train station where we could get a cheap meal. The station reminded me of the old Greyhound bus station I'd been stranded in one night just a few years before in June 1968 in downtown Portland, Oregon.

It was a semi-dark train station where we bought bratwurst sausages and beers and sat down at a table to eat and drink. The Nuremburg train station was open to the homeless and the drunken derelicts, just like the Portland Greyhound bus station I'd experienced a few years earlier. It wasn't long before a drunk staggered toward us and sat down at our table, so we gulped down our sausages and beers and left. We drove outside town, found a place to pull over in a forested area, and slept that night in the car.

We were on the *autobahn* headed south for Munich the next day when, along the way, I noticed a road sign that read, "Dachau Concentration Camp Memorial Site–5 KM." I told Randy and Bill I wanted to stop and visit this Holocaust Memorial site. It was about a year before this time when I came into Long Binh Post on my daily ambulance run to the 584th to pick up our mail; in the office I'd noticed a card-box full of paperbacks that had been shipped to us by the USO. I picked up a book that seemed interesting *The Pawn Broker*. This book tells the story of Sol Nazerman, a holocaust concentration camp survivor, who suffers flashbacks of his past Nazi imprisonment as he tries to cope with his daily life operating a pawnshop in East Harlem in New York City. I returned to Bearcat with it and became absorbed in it.

While my experiences in Vietnam were nothing compared to what Sol experienced, I could relate in some ways to what he went through. While living in the camps in Vietnam I was always aware of the underlying presence of death around me. I could feel it. It was in the air. I could smell it. I could breathe it. It was the smell of blood mixed with the smell of mud. Death was everywhere all the time. I have, since those days, felt a special bond and understanding with holocaust survivors. I understand it. Randy, Bill, and I entered the Dachau Memorial site, took the tour, went through the barracks and saw the cremation ovens where tens of thousands of Jews and others met their fate and were murdered. Such an unbelievably sad place. We paid our respects, then left.

We continued south into the Bavarian capital city of Munich. Arriving later that afternoon, we checked into an inexpensive hotel, then immediately made our way to the notorious Munich *Hofbräuhaus* beer hall, for a night of wild beer drinking and merriment. The Munich *Hofbräuhaus* is a huge, cavernous German-food and drinking hall where robust maids, carry beer steins to rows and rows of tourists sitting at long tables to a background of *Oom-Pah-Pah* music. Bill, Randy, and I found a table and began our drinking journey. The beer steins each held a liter of delicious German beer, and we drank one liter after another.

Not long after we sat down, we noticed three young, attractive, American tourist girls had sat down at a table close to ours, so I got up and invited them to join us at our table. They accepted. We were all carrying on well and having a good time when we were interrupted by a group of three or four American Army soldiers who barged into our scene at the table and started making moves on the chicks. This really pissed me off. The girls weren't digging them either. These guys were coming off like true American Army ground-pounding drunk jerks. They had to go. I took on the guy who looked like their leader and asked him to stand up there at the table where we were sitting. I told him in very blunt terms that the women were turned off by him and his rude buddies and that they had to go.

He stared at me and said, "Well, Mother-Fucker, what if we don't want to do that? What if we don't want to go? What in the fuck are you going to do about it?"

Randy, Bill, and the three girls were sitting tensely watching this all go down. This guy was nothing but an Army punk. I looked at him calmly and said,

"These girls don't want you bugging them. It's obvious. Do you understand what I'm telling you?"

He repeated, "So what are you going to do about it, Mother-Fucker?"

By this time people at the surrounding tables had taken notice of the situation and became concerned. It was quite a scene. He challenged me loudly one more time.

"Well, Mother-Fucker, what are you going to do about it?"

I burrowed into his mind with a serious intent and told him,

"Do you know what? These girls don't want you here and we don't want you and your buddies here either. Nobody wants you here. Now you may not like this, and you may try to punch me in the nose or something like that, but you've got to know that I will also punch you in the nose and it may start bleeding all over the place and I am sure that you won't like that either. Got this?"

He responded, "You going to punch me in the nose? I don't think so!"

I responded, starring him down, "Okay, wanna try me? I think it could easily happen."

I went on to further explain my feelings to him,

"Look ... neither you nor I want to get into this, right? This beer hall is an enormous place, big enough for all of us to have a great time tonight, right? So why spoil it when we can all just have fun? Just move on and let's all get on and enjoy ourselves, okay?"

He looked away and motioned to his buddies. They then respectfully got up and left the table. One of the girls got up immediately and gave me a deep and wet tongue kiss as a thank you for my bravery. I wasn't really as brave and macho as my act pretended to be... but it worked. The party started again with great relief, and we all drank and sang and partied ourselves into oblivion.

We were three young American white guys traveling free and on the run throughout the continent without a care in the world except to have a great time. We'd brought along a large pocketful of hashish, which we'd gotten from a street vendor outside of an all-night underground hashish nightclub in Berlin just before we left. This would keep us high throughout most of our trip. Driving through Austria, Switzerland, and Italy, we would often stop along the way at roadside stands to buy fresh fruit, bread, cheese, and sausage, and enormous bottles of the best red wine imaginable for fifty cents a bottle. These were the staples that kept us going, and we were happily satisfied and stoned most of the time. Bill's early fifties vintage four-door Mercedes sedan became our traveling home away from home, our RV, and our best friend, so we gave the car a name. He became known to the three of us as "Carl-Heinze," and we loved him as if he were one of us.

From Munich we travelled south through Austria and into Switzerland. We drove into the mountains but discovered the roads were closed. There was no way to cross the Alps by car because huge snowdrifts and ice had closed off all the roads. We came back down into a valley and discovered a train station loading cars up onto flatcars, getting ready to ship them by rail to Italy, entirely through the Alps via an underground tunnel. We paid the fare and drove Carl-Heinze up onto the flatcar, not knowing what to expect. They instructed us to put on the parking brake and stay inside the car and not get out.

After about an hour of traveling through this dark mountain train tunnel, we arrived and came out into a completely different world of sunshine. It was glorious. We drove to the small Swiss-Italian town of San Bernardino. Then, from the mountains, we drove south into the northern Italian capital city of Milano, arriving late that night. With maps, we navigated to the central part of the city and found a bar/café that was open all night where we got pizza and drank beer. We then got back into the car and headed out along the highway to find a place in the countryside to lay out our sleeping bags and get some sleep. We were exhausted. I woke up on the ground not long after that, with the sun coming up, and the sound of a farm tractor approaching me. We'd laid out our sleeping bags and camped in a farmer's cornfield, and he didn't appreciate us being there. We hurriedly packed up our things and hit the road again. This was a magical time. A young traveler's paradise, it was rich to be out there on the road without a care in the world, enjoying every day that was so filled with new discoveries.

We continued south, visiting Venice and Ravenna, camping along the way, then down the Adriatic coast of Italy all the way through Bari and into the port city of Brindisi. This is where we loaded Carl-Heinze onto a ferry ship to carry us over the Adriatic Sea and deliver us to the northern coast of Greece. Our ship arrived late in the afternoon at the small Grecian port town of Igoumenitsa. We drove the car off the dock and approached a Greek customs check point.Waiting to inspect us at the checkpoint were these country bumpkin-looking Greek military guys with the usual complement of assault weapons hanging from their belts and shoulders.

Bill, Randy, and I had been out on the road for a while, cruising and not worrying about a thing—just enjoying it all. We were so relaxed that we kept our hash-pipe right up on the dashboard in plain sight. Suddenly, realizing our situation, I called out to Randy, who was riding shotgun, to hand the hash and pipe to me. Bill was driving, and I was in the backseat. I quickly hid them. The officials on duty inspected our passports, looked us over, noting Bill's US Air Force license plates. They then immediately passed us through their checkpoint with no problem. With great relief, we'd made it through.

We travelled down the Adriatic coast of Greece, camping

along the way, then came into Athens where we spent several days touring the city; walking around its Acropolis and other magnificent, historic sights. Then it was back, via car-ferry again, to southern Italy, where we visited Naples and the incredible ruins of Pompeii. In Rome we stayed in a cheap hotel for 2 days and nights exploring the city's Colosseum, many museums, and its nightlife; then on to Marseille, along the Mediterranean coast France, and finally west to Barcelona, Spain, where we took in a bullfight and stayed for a few days.

It was nearly time for Bill's thirty-day military leave to be over, so we chartered a path north, staying over in Paris for a while, before heading back to Berlin. I had many wonderful and unforgettable experiences along the way during this healing European journey. After living in Hell for the previous two years of my life in the Army and in Vietnam, this trip to Europe was one of the best life decisions I'd ever made. It helped to clear my head out; to release so much.

CHAPTER FORTY-EIGHT

Six Dollars in My Wallet

IT WAS ON a hot, mid-July evening in 1970 when I returned to the United States and landed at JFK Airport in New York City. I had just six American dollars in my wallet and a pocketful of useless European coins. I had nothing at all besides that; no credit cards or anything else of value, except a backpack and a sleeping bag. I had no ticket home.

The night before my flight, I'd slept on the ground in a beautiful, forested area within walking distance to the entrance of the Luxembourg International Airport. It was a free space to lay out a sleeping bag. During those times countries allowed us to do these kinds of things. Hippies were freely carrying on, with music and all. They were mostly, just like me, young American kids waiting to fly back home to America from a summer of European adventures. I laid there on the ground and peacefully went to sleep.

In the early morning I got up and made my way to check in at the Luxembourg international terminal. It wasn't long before I took my seat on a plane loaded with young traveling vagabonds like me; all headed back to America. There was a young guy seated next to me on the flight who I began a friendly conversation with. He was a Yale college student about my age who'd also been traveling Europe as I had during that summer. We had stories to share with one another about our experiences during our travels. His name was Roger. Our plane landed at JFK and we disembarked. I had no idea where I was going to go or what I was going to do; I had no money and no ticket to get back to California from New York City. There were lots of young people like me who were just hanging out at the airport waiting to make their connections. Many of us were voyagers who had not made definite plans for anything. We were just "On the Road" in those days.

I met a girl in the airport and we started talking. Lisa had also just come off a plane from Europe and was wondering how in the hell she was going to make it back home to St. Louis. Like me, she was stranded in the terminal at JFK with no money; with nothing at all but her backpack and a sleeping bag and wondering what she was going to do. We soon realized we were in the same boat and I told her my plan was to wait there in the airport that night until the sun came up, then to walk out and hitchhike my way home to California. I told her if she wanted to join me, we could team up and hitchhike together all the way to St. Louis. Lisa liked the idea of the adventure and accepted my proposal. So that was our plan, to hit the road together.

We sat down on a bench in the terminal and waited. It was getting late, and we were both getting hungry, so I went to a snack stand and bought us hot dogs and chips. This cost me four dollars. The terminal was crowded with throngs of young people like ourselves, coming and going, either taking off for or returning home from Europe. While sitting on the bench eating our hot dogs, a flight arrived and its disembarking passengers emerged from the gate, streaming by us, heading for their connecting flights. Suddenly a young woman approached us and said, "Lisa! What are you doing here?"

Lisa said, "Maria! What are *you* doing here?"

They were old high school classmates in St. Louis. Lisa explained to Maria that she had just arrived there at JFK from an incredible summer in Europe and, because she had no ticket home, was planning to hitchhike, as soon as the sun came up, from New York City all the way back to St. Louis. She introduced me to Maria,

"Maria, this is Jim."

Maria told Lisa, "I don't think this is a very good idea."

Lisa replied that she had no ticket home and was completely broke, so hitchhiking home was her only option. Maria told Lisa that she had plenty of money and was getting ready to board a flight home to St. Louis that would be taking off soon and she would buy Lisa a ticket to join her on that same flight if she wanted.

Lisa said, "I don't know, Maria. I've already promised Jim here I would hitchhike across the country with him."

Maria replied, "Don't be silly Lisa, you know that that would be entirely too dangerous."

I'd been standing there listening to the conversation when I interrupted and said to Lisa, "You know, if it was me, Lisa, I would accept Maria's offer."

Maria immediately reached into her purse and pulled out a twenty-dollar bill and pressed it into my hand and said, "Thank you, Jim, for realizing what's best for Lisa. I wish you well on your journey home."

It was getting close to midnight. I walked back to the area where I'd originally met Lisa and sat down in a stairwell crowded with dozens of young travelers with backpacks like myself who were crisscrossing the country and the world, seeking adventure. I took a seat and realized I was sitting right next to Roger, the guy I had sat next to on the flight from Luxembourg. He was asleep and gently snoring. After a while, he woke up, and we began talking again.

Roger was in the same situation as I. He had no money and no way to get back home. In those days we didn't have credit or debit cards, and all transactions were cash. If you were to pay for or buy anything, you would have to pull out your wallet and pay for it in cash. During our flight, Roger had explained to me he was a student living in New Haven, Connecticut, and had an apartment there. He went on and on about how great it was to be a student there in New Haven with Yale and all. An exciting place.

He asked what my plans were, and I told him I intended to leave the JFK terminal as soon as the sun came up to begin my trip hitchhiking across America. I asked him what his plans were, and he told me he didn't know how he was going to get home to New Haven because he was stranded at the airport with no money. He then invited me to come up to his place in Connecticut, if possible, to stay with him for a while and I accepted his offer. The question then was how we were going to get to New Haven from JFK?

We walked over to a travel window and found an agent who told us there was a private limousine that would soon leave the airport bound for New Haven. Roger and I looked at each other. How much would the fare be? The clerk told us that the fare would be $11 for each of us. Twenty-two dollars in total. When I had flown into JFK, I had just six dollars in my wallet. That was my total worth. I'd spent four dollars on hot dogs and chips earlier for Lisa and I and that had left me with only two dollars. Then Lisa's friend arrived and forced a twenty spot on me; this left me with twenty-two dollars. At that moment I realized that somehow, magically, I had the exact cash in my wallet we needed. I winked at Roger and told him I had our fare covered. I bought our tickets and we climbed into the back of a long, black Cadillac limousine for a two-hour long cruise up north from JFK to downtown New Haven, Connecticut. It was just the two of us being driven by a uniformed chauffeur.

Arriving in central New Haven at about two in the morning, we came to an all-night dinner; the White Castle Restaurant. Roger told me he knew the night manager there and that she would be glad to serve us all the burgers and fries we wanted for free. When we walked inside, I was startled a bit that nearly all the counter stools were taken up in the dim light by gorgeous Black transvestites in full drag. I was back in America and back in hamburger heaven once again.

Roger generously took me in and offered food and lodging for a few days in his downtown apartment in New Haven, but I knew I had to find some way to earn my keep before I hit the road. I found employment for a day at a daily hire place that deployed me and another guy, a Black guy, to work in a boxcar sitting on a rail in an industrial area of New Haven. All day long I labored with him, to lift one hundred-pound bags of starch out of the boxcar onto a truck. He took one end of the bag and I lifted the other. Fifty pounds each. We did this labor for eight hours straight without let-up. The New England heat and humidity in the boxcar in mid-July were stifling and left us both exhausted and drenched in sweat when it was over. All of this effort and just thirteen dollars to show for it at the end of the day.

That evening, Roger, a few of his friends, and I took off and went to a bar in New Haven where we got pizza. Then we went to a swinging nightclub where we smoked and drank beer and boogied the night away, dancing to great live rock-and-roll, and soul, music. It was all so much fun, but that evening I spent every last penny of the money I had so slavishly earned that day.

Within a few weeks of living with Roger in New Haven, I was able to hire out my labor and earn enough money to leave and head out on my westward journey home. With less than fifty dollars in my pocket I hit the road with my backpack and sleeping bag to hitch-hike across America. This hitch-hiking trip became my own epic Jack Kerouac, *On the Road* experience, an incredible journey loaded with stories of being out there on a road of danger and adventure.

CHAPTER FORTY-NINE

A Canadian Dream

I HITCHED WEST from New Haven, Connecticut, crossed the Hudson River, and started making my way north through the highways and byways of the countryside of upstate New York. I camped alone off deserted mountain roads in the Adirondacks and felt at peace. Caught a ride that took me all the way to Buffalo. I still had the address of my old friend, Janis Crosby, in my wallet. The last letter I'd received from her was mailed from somewhere in Toronto, Canada, so I decided I would try to find and reconnect with her there. The city of Toronto is just north of Buffalo and Niagara Falls and Lake Ontario. I figured I could easily cross the US/Canada border there, then camp and hitch my way up into Toronto so that I could look up Janis. I had been travelling throughout Europe for months in this manner, going along, entering one country after another with no difficulties at all and assumed crossing the border from the US into Canada would be the same. I had this idea that Canada was a much more civilized and welcoming place than the United States.

It was late in the afternoon when my ride dropped me off at the "Peace Bridge" which spans the Niagara River in Buffalo, New York. He dropped me off at the bridge with my backpack where I picked it up and began the long trudge across the bridge into Canada and the Canadian customs checkpoint. Looking pretty scruffy after months of living on the road I entered the customs office and laid down my backpack, took out my passport and expected to be passed through with no hassle. Instead, I received a hostile reception. They instructed me to take every item out of my backpack for display and inspection. One of the first questions I was asked was how much money I had with me.

I replied, "Thirty-five dollars...US"

The female customs inspector then told me that backpacking riffraff like myself with nothing were not welcomed into Canada and that I must pack up my belongings and make my way back over the "Peace Bridge" to America where I'd come from. I did so. I was humiliated and furious as I made my way back over the bridge. I was also determined to get across the border in some other way. After walking back over to the US side, I located a spot on the road where motorists were lining up to cross the bridge and enter Canada. I put out my thumb and soon a car pulled over. A guy got out, opened his trunk and, in a friendly manner, told me to throw my backpack in and join him. I thanked him and relayed to him the experience I'd just had trying to cross the border. He said not to worry about a thing. He was headed for Toronto to attend his sister's wedding and that if the border officials asked any questions, he would just tell them I was his longtime friend from back home in Texas who also wanted to attend the wedding.

We crossed the bridge and drove up to the checkpoint official standing there who asked what business we had for entering Canada. The guy told her we were on our way to Toronto to see his sister get married there. She then asked him to open up his trunk. He did so. She inspected then asked,

"Is one of you a hitchhiker?" Of course, we said no. She then instructed us to drive the car to the side and enter the inspections office which we did. We got out of the car and walked into the inspector's office where we were met by two burly Canadian Border Custom's guards, standing behind a counter. They greeted us with threatening expressions. This was when the interrogations began.

These assholes were really having fun with the situation as they knew the score and had been watching me and waiting for me. The first thing they demanded was for us to hand over our IDs. The poor guy who picked me up didn't have his wallet in his pocket, so they looked at my ID, then asked the driver to tell them, since I was such a good friend of his, what my full name was. The game was over. They took him away somewhere, then locked painful handcuffs on my wrists and jerked me to a dark jail cell. Within an hour, I was led into a darkened room where I was placed on a high stool with my hands locked behind my back. Over my head hung a bright light-bulb and in front of me sat four very intimidating looking Canadian "Mounties" with their silly-looking "Bobby" hats and uniforms and all, trying their best to be really tough guys.

The interrogation began.

"So, who are you and where do you come from and why are you trying to sneak into Canada?"

I responded, "My name is James Simpson Gibson, and I am from Anaheim, California, in the United States. I am not trying to *sneak* into Canada but only trying to visit an old girlfriend of mine, a Canadian citizen, who I believe lives in Toronto. That's it."

One of them threatened, "We've had enough of you, American hippie trash, coming here into our country trying to escape your country's service in Vietnam. Your type has become a huge drain on our nation's economy, and we're done with all that. We know what you bums are all about and we are going to deport you. That means you're our prisoner now and we shall have fun with you in our prisons for few weeks before we let you go. What do you think of that? Do you understand?"

It was at this point I thought a bit about my situation and put on a very convincing act. I cleverly broke down and cried and begged for mercy. I told them I was not one of those bums trying to get into Canada trying to escape serving my country in Vietnam because I had already done my time in Vietnam as a medical corpsman on the ground there and had been honorably discharged from the United States Army. This made a big impact upon them. They were impressed. They questioned me extensively to make sure my story was on the level, then took the cuffs off me and led me out to a room where I could pick up my backpack. They warned me to not try to come back to Canada for a long time. Once again, I made my way back over the Peace Bridge toward Buffalo. So much for The Canadian Dream.

CHAPTER FIFTY

Tragedy at Home

IT TOOK ME a couple weeks to hitch-hike across America. I was lean, exhausted, and weary from being out there on the road; worn out from sleeping under bridges and trying to survive the dangerous journey. It was a warm summer evening in late 1970 when I arrived at my parent's home there in Anaheim. I rang their doorbell, and once again, they generously took me in.

Arriving just in time to enroll in college for the fall semester, I went back to school to begin receiving veteran's G.I. Bill educational benefit checks in the mail. My father and I became closer friends during this time, spending long hours together in the late nights drinking and sharing our life experiences; he, sipping on shots of Jim Beam and I sipping on a beer and smoking cigarettes. We talked about our war experiences. His experiences, a generation before in the South Pacific with the Navy during the extremely violent war with Japan, and mine with the Army in Vietnam. We'd both been through our own versions of hell, survived and made it home alive. Not only that, he, as a young man, had once hitchhiked and travelled west from Oklahoma to California as a poor Okie vagabond, in much the same way I had just hitchhiked across

America. I got to know him much better and learned to love him despite our differences.

|||

"Call an ambulance!"

I yelled this out to my mom and my brother Bill from the hall in our family home. I'd discovered Dad choking and gasping as he lay there in his bed. He'd suffered a massive life-ending stroke and died right there. His death was completely unexpected; He was so young, only fifty-five.

Losing Dad was devasting for us all. We went through the usual funeral process. The next day, after the funeral, I took off to the mountains in my old station wagon and camped by myself in the forest for several days and nights, contemplating. I spent my time alone, fasting, only drinking water. I'd been through and learned so much in my short life. As I sat there on the mountainside in the stillness and beauty the pine forest that surrounded me, I gave thanks for the my survival and all that life had given me. I decided to continue on.

CHAPTER FIFTY–ONE

Happier Days

FOUR YEARS HAD gone by since the first time I enrolled in college, and there I was again, on the that very same campus, Fullerton Junior College; rediscovering once again, how much I enjoyed learning. I declared an art major and loved my classes, especially my art classes. It was then I began painting in oils. An old run-down five-story, brick, and mortar office building, "The Wilshire Building" stood in downtown Fullerton, and offered live-in studios to art students for only forty dollars a month. I rented one, moved in, and set up my easel. Life was good to me then and I was grateful. This time was a relief from the misery I'd experienced in the intervening years; the war and my father's death. It had been almost a year since I had returned from the war, and I was finally feeling as though I was adjusting and fitting in.

My good fortune continued when I met Gale. I was a lonely, young, Vietnam Veteran recovering from undiagnosed PTSD, and she was a young, beautiful woman trying to escape an unhappy family situation. I loved her from the very first time I saw her. We were both innocents trying to escape the crazy world around us. Before we knew it, Gale was pregnant. We weren't expecting this or ready for this, so I asked her if this was what she really wanted– if she wanted to have the baby? She answered that without question she was going to have the baby, so I told her that, without question I would take care of her and become the baby's father. This was a time of serious change for both of us. I had gone through the war, the traveling and everything, and had been goofing off. Now those days were over, and it was time for me to settle down and get serious about life. I had to figure out how to support a family. Neither of us wanted to get married and I told Gale we could just live together and that I would take care of everything without us having to get married. She told me her dad would not consent to this, and we had to get married if we were to live together.

So, we got married. One day we took the bus to the county courthouse in downtown Inglewood and asked the presiding judge to marry us on his lunch break. Gale cried during the ceremony. I didn't want to do it either, but we got married anyway just to please her parents. I knew that whatever the outcome, I would do my best to be the best husband and father I could be.

But how was I going to make a living for us? What were my employable skills? The only thing I really knew how to do was what I'd done in Vietnam: drive an ambulance. I visited local ambulance companies and applied for employment. I soon found out that the ambulance companies during this time only required a very simple certification from the American Red Cross Society, and in order to get this certification I had to attend and sit through several Red Cross medical education classes and then pass their tests. I did so. Gale wanted to stay close to her family in Inglewood, so I applied for a job as an ambulance attendant with a company there and was hired. I found a tiny but nice duplex apartment nearby for us to move into and prepare our nest for our children on the way. In January 1972, my daughter, Annie, was born. A year and a half later my son John came along. In no time, I was married with two kids. Despite the unhappy beginnings of our marriage, those times with the births of our children, were the happiest days of my life.

CHAPTER FIFTY-TWO

Los Angeles Ambulance Story

INGLEWOOD IS AN incorporated city within the immense metropolitan region of Los Angeles. Some neighborhoods are well kept, safe and middle class, but there are many that are dangerous. It borders South Central LA where gangs organize to rule the streets and it can be a violent place. I went to work as an ambulance attendant that summer, for an ambulance company located in Inglewood.

The McDougal family that owned the ambulance company was a well tied-in Inglewood family who also owned and operated a very prominent mortuary in the city. The mortuary which stood out distinctly on one of the more prominent avenues of Inglewood resembled a large white southern plantation style mansion, with twenty-foot high columns. It was like something straight out of the deep south. The McDougal Ambulance Company operated its business out of the back of this mortuary.

In the fifties and sixties after World War II, Los Angeles went through a major racial transition. During those years, many African American families began moving out of the racially divided southern states, where there was little opportunity for them, to places out west like Los Angeles. Many of them came to live in the southern neighborhoods of Los Angeles, in places like Compton and Inglewood. Until the end of WWII and into the early sixties, Inglewood was regarded as a solidly white middle-class suburb of LA. It was a place of palm trees near to the South Bay beaches where you could expect to send your white kids to the finest public schools and maybe even live across the street from one of the families of the Beach Boys. Gale's family lived right across the street from Mike Love's family.

It was in the latter fifties when African Americans bought houses and moved into the area when something known as "White Flight" began happen in Inglewood. White families, one neighborhood after another, put their houses up for sale and moved away to "safe" places that were still white, like Orange County or "The Valley." In 1971, when I moved into the little duplex in Inglewood and began working for the ambulance company, things were tense. The dynamics of the community were changing from an old entitled and entrenched white class, accustomed to having its way, to a new situation where white people were becoming a minority, encircled by a Black majority. Though they still owned and controlled the wealth and the reins of power, families like the McDougals were having a tough time accepting and dealing with the changes.

While working for them as an attendant on one of their ambulance crews, I noticed an undercurrent of racism in the company. Not wanting to hire Blacks to work for them, they hired working-class white guys to work for them like servants They worked us night and day, twenty-four hours on and twenty-four hours off; seven days a week without letup and paid us a pittance. There were no benefits. The twenty-four hours on were mostly constant with little or no breaks for rest or sleep between calls. The twenty-four hours off were hours where we would rest up and try to reconstitute ourselves for the next twenty-four hours on. This was a horrible job, but it was all I had. They provided us uniforms of white-collared shirts, emblazoned with their company's green logos, and matching dark green slacks. We were required to launder and iron these uniforms at our expense. All so the company's public image could shine while we drove around the city in their long, sleek, brand-new, green, and white hearse-like Cadillac ambulances. In between calls we were required to wash, wax, and polish the chrome of these vehicles. Such was the state of first responder service in those times, before the public system of fire department paramedics replaced companies like this.

After a few months working for these assholes, I put in an application to work at the Los Angeles County USC Medical Center. My application was accepted, and I was relieved to be out of that dead-end ambulance job. I was to begin my employment with the County on October 8, so this left me with nearly three weeks to creatively think and consider ways I was going to quit and pay back the boss and his company—the racist, assholes, who had been using and abusing me as their employee.

The owner's youngest son, Jason, was an obnoxious, pudgy, pimply-faced punk; an eighteen-year-old with no life experience who had been given the job of night dispatcher by his father. They put him in charge of us older guys at night, and we all knew what the score was and resented that his father had placed him in authority over us. One night my partner and I, trying to relax from a hard day of non-stop calls, were trying to get a brief rest when we were awakened by the punk who called us. He explained to us we were to respond to a local nursing home and pick up an elderly woman complaining of chest pains and that we were to deliver her to a nearby hospital emergency room. He then clearly stated –

"If this woman is a nigger and her family are niggers, then I want payment from them up front before we transport them!"

My partner, Allen, asked for clarification and the reply was once again –

"If this woman is a nigger and her family are niggers, then I want payment from them up front!"

We drove to the nursing home, came into the patient's room, and found the woman there who was in distress. The elderly Black woman was lying in her bed with her daughter and a few other family members by her bedside. She was having trouble breathing. We ignored Jason's racist order, placed an oxygen canula in her nose, and immediately lifted her onto our gurney and transported her to a nearby hospital where we brought her into the ER. When we arrived at the hospital, the medical staff responded, and we transferred her from our ambulance gurney onto one of their beds. The ER nurses then closed the curtain around the patient where they and the attendant ER Doc began to diagnose and take care of her. The old woman's daughter and another relative were also there behind the curtain. Allen and I had delivered the elderly Black woman to the hospital and not demanded money from her in advance, as the boss's son had instructed us to do. We were folding up our ambulance gurney, standing just outside the closed patient curtain, when something came to me. I just couldn't take it anymore.

I had a sudden epiphany. My new job with the County was lined up and I had been wondering just exactly how I was going to announce to this abusive, racist, asshole, ambulance company that I would no longer be working for them. Standing there, I realized how I was going to quit my job. In an earlier chapter in this book, I told the story of an experience of mine that occurred one day during Army basic training. I described how an answer had just come to me as if out of the blue; an answer that became the perfect solution to my problem.

Standing in the hospital ER that night a similar response came to me; once again, from somewhere deep within my soul. In a booming voice, I yelled out to my partner, "Hey Allen! Aren't we supposed to be charging these BLACK PEOPLE in advance and up front for their ambulance transportation costs?"

Everything went silent in the emergency room. Everyone had heard what I said. There were gasps. You could have heard a pin drop. Immediately came the sound of the curtain being swung open from the exam room and the old woman's daughter was standing there, staring at me with an intense burning hatred in her eyes. I looked straight back at her and held out my right index finger, beckoning her to come forward. She did so. I then asked her to step outside the ER with me for a moment.

I explained it all to her. I told her the reasons for what I'd done and explained to her that what I'd yelled out was true. Those were our orders from our employer and that was the way he operated the company. I apologized for any upset I caused to her, her mother, and her family, and also told her I felt that it was my moral and ethical duty to let her and her family know what was going on. She responded to me with absolute gratitude for what I had done and said she understood it all very well. Then she told me her son-in-law was a well-connected NAACP (National Association for the Advancement of Colored People) attorney whose office was located in the LA area, and that she would notify him about all that had just taken place. She said she was sure there would be consequences and changes. We shook hands, hugged each other, and said good night.

I came back into the ER where Allen was standing in shock with a *what the fuck* expression on his face. Soon the ER Charge Nurse came up to us, enraged, telling me she was going to immediately report what I had done to my employer, and that I would never, ever, be allowed to enter that ER again. I just looked at her, smiled, and calmly said, "Well fine, why don't you just do whatever you have to do?"

We took the gurney back out to the ambulance, stowed it away, and sat in the cab in the hospital parking lot, lit up cigarettes and began talking. I explained to Allen what I'd done, but he was almost speechless. We waited in the parking lot for another fifteen minutes when we got the call to immediately return to the station. We were advised to stay in the barracks and not come out until the morning shift change. When the sun came up and our crew replacements arrived, I got up off my cot, gathered my things, and casually strolled across the parking lot into the mortuary business office. I was met by one of the more superior company bosses who told me I was to leave the premises right away. I said, "OK, this means I'm fired, right?"

He just nodded and said, "Please leave now."

I responded, "But what about the pay the company owes me?"

He told me I could come back to the office the next day to pick up my check. I picked up my stuff, got on my bicycle, then rode home in the early morning sun. I didn't even have the means in those days to afford a car, but I had a wide grin on my face as I rode along, thrilled to get away from those assholes and start a new direction. Some might ask why I did this since I had already found a new job and arranged to leave the company. A few months later I went out one night and cruised by one of the donut shops in the neighborhood where we would hang out in our ambulance between calls. I saw a Black guy sitting behind the wheel of the ambulance. People's Justice.

CHAPTER FIFTY–THREE

The Burn Ward

I REPORTED TO my new job as a Hospital Corpsman at the huge Los Angeles County USC Medical Center. The hospital, built in 1933, is a massive concrete structure, a twenty-story, Art Deco-style monolith on a hill over-looking the city of Los Angeles; one of the biggest buildings, in terms of square footage, in the entire world. This Medical Center treated more patients in a single year than any other medical system in the United States, other than Metro in New York City, or Cook County in Chicago. It was a gigantic medical system with several interlocking specialist hospitals employing over sixty-thousand doctors, nurses, health workers, and other employees.

The County wanted to upgrade its Burn Center, so they brought on board one of the country's foremost burn care surgeons to head up its program and serve as its Chief of Staff. Dr. Bruce Smith had recently been discharged from the US Army's Medical Corps where he had headed up the Army's burn care program during the last years of the Vietnam War. He was one of the world's leading burn care specialists. The County promised just about anything to him he wanted to transform the LA County Burn Center into one of the country's finest. He had them construct an entirely new and completely sealed off burn ward on the 12th floor of the hospital; this was to become a state-of-the-art facility complete with its own ER, ICU, Surgery, Lab, and Pharmacy. Everything. They also allowed him to hire recently returned military medical corpsmen to work there on his new burn ward with him. From his experiences in the Army, he had a lot of confidence in, and appreciation for, our abilities. To suit his request, the County created an entirely new medical job category for us, "Hospital Corpsman." He wanted to train returning medics to become burn care specialists. This new position offered a good salary and generous benefits.

One day I found myself sitting in a chair being interviewed by a panel comprised of the hospital administration, the nursing staff, and Dr. Smith. Dr. Smith asked if I had any personal experiences caring for burn victims. I told them I had. I described to them my first experience with burn victims. This had occurred on a day early in my Vietnam War tour in a field hospital. I was standing there in a hallway one day when someone yelled,

"Open the doors, we have to bring these soldiers through!"

To my horror, two young men on gurneys, burned beyond recognition, were being wheeled through the halls. They were still alive and cognizant of their condition. They looked like dark strips of crispy bacon with their arms outstretched on their gurneys. Their eyes were nothing but pools of pus. As I assisted them through the swinging doorways, I was afraid that if I'd allowed it the doors might have just broken off. In fact, the Army Doctors and nurses that worked there had become so emotionally hardened by these horrific cases that they sometimes referred to these burn victims as "Crispy Critters." My story caused Dr. Smith, and the rest of the panel to sit up and take notice. I also told them the story of the young Vietnamese boy who was badly burned while burning our shit out there at Bearcat one day, and how we took him in and cared for him, and healed him of his injuries. They hired me. Within a year, the LA County USC Burn Center became renowned as one of the nation's leading burn care centers. I worked there mostly in the Intensive Care Unit on the night shift for the next six years.

I took my job seriously and gained my supervisor's attention as I became an expert in all aspects of burn care, especially as a respiratory and ventilator specialist. This room was like no other place in the world with its morbidity rate of forty percent. These patients usually died in the most agonizing ways. Working there was like working deep within the belly of the modern medical beast where four out of ten patients would leave the ICU in the plastic shrouds that I or other nurses would wrap them in. Children died on me. Men. Women. Young and old people died on me. Every age. Every description of a human being died on me. They were mostly poor, mostly Black or brown, but not only. We were the busiest burn center in the nation, and I dealt with it all. Dealt with it with my hands, with my body, mind and soul— hundreds of deaths of the worst kind imaginable. All of this took an enormous toll on me. I would arrive home at around midnight, often with the smell of burnt human flesh permeating my clothing, hair, and body. I always took a shower.

During this time in my life, I focused my energy on trying to help as many people and their families as I could, to get through the most trying times of their lives. Looking back on it all, I realize that my employment in the burn ward was a psychological buffer. It was a transition between the horrors of my Vietnam experiences and the every-day normal experiences of existence in "The World." This very intense environment of death and trauma enabled me to relate to something I was familiar with. It allowed me to focus my energies and realize my worth and contribution to society. For ten years, I existed in this way. From the age of twenty until thirty, my life had been engulfed in a reality of death and dying.

One day I decided I'd had enough, and I just didn't want to have any more to do with it. It was an abrupt decision I made not to report for work one evening. I didn't even call in. The next morning I went in and handed in my resignation.

CHAPTER FIFTY-FOUR

Breaking Down

AFTER I LEFT the burn ward I fell apart mentally for a while. That which had sufficed to provide a sense of stability in my life was now gone and I felt everything was coming undone. I began to experience anxiety and depression. Insomnia and chronic fatigue led to an overall inability to cope with the most basic things. I felt I was going crazy. I sought help from professional therapists several times but received absolutely no relief because I had no health insurance or any way to pay them. Everything was coming apart and I was on my own.

I had no other way to make a living. How was I going to take care of my family now? I had no civilian medical license or any other credentials or experience to fall back on. What was I going to do? I'd lost everything. I was desperate. Not knowing what else to do, I enrolled in a local community college and took up a trade. I studied printing technology, took a few classes, and applied myself to the best of my abilities. I was living hand to mouth in those days and trying to provide for my family at the same time. The stress was tearing my marriage apart. My car's engine blew up and I had no money to fix it. I would get up early in the morning, then ride to the college on my bicycle to attend classes. At noon I would switch from the bicycle and take a two-hour bus ride through Orange County into Santa Ana, where I would punch a time clock to begin my minimum wage night shift printing factory job beginning at 2 pm. At 11pm, I would hitchhike my way home on the freeway. This went on for months.

The job was as an apprentice, in a printing factory, where I made just barely enough, with the aid of public food stamps, to provide for my family with only the most rudimentary level of subsistence. The stress of all this was hard to take and tearing me to the bone. I went through several dead-end printing jobs where I would either quit or get fired. These printing companies were mostly small, family businesses whose owners felt entitled, like little bourgeois kings and queens, who looked down upon and usually treated their employees like shit. Most of us were wage, time-clock slaves, just barely getting by on our measly pay to pay the bills and our landlords their rents. Most workers have a sense that they are getting screwed by the system, but are trained from the moment of birth to ignore it. Most of us just wanted to fit in and get by somehow.

This miserable life that I was experiencing continued for a few years until I grew tired of it; I started a process of re-examining and reclaiming my existence. I began a rigorous physical workout program and took classes in meditation and martial arts. I also involved myself in political activism. In time I shifted my attention from the physical and the meditative and martial arts stuff. and became more interested and involved with the political.

It was in 1979 when I came full-circle, back to my earlier understanding of things. I realized once again that my misery was entirely of a political-economic nature. My reclamation of myself was now underway; this was the recognition of the basic truth that controlled my life. The truth that it's all about the money; about who controls it; it's about who owns whom. It's about the brutality of the predominant economic system we all live under; the dog-eat-dog system of Capitalism. I knew I was being eaten alive by it.

Early in this book I wrote about the things that had influenced and shaped my mind as a young man, especially the writings of Jack London, which led me into the study of Socialism. While going through high school I had realized all of this, but the draft and the Vietnam War had gotten in the way and the difficulties of surviving in this world and trying to hold on and raise a family had clouded my consciousness from what was really going on. The war and the years of working in the burn ward and everything else took its toll on me. It took years, but I eventually found my way back.

CHAPTER FIFTY-FIVE

Breaking Free

IT WAS AFTER being fired from a job in 1979 that I finally threw off the yoke and rebelled. I rebelled once again against The System as I had done in those years before I'd been drafted; before all the shit began. I grew my hair long and got fired from other jobs as well; throwing myself in the face of anyone foolish enough to hire me. I was on fire and I had a great time just fucking with people's heads. I loved toying with their minds. I became "crazy" again, but this time my craziness was intentional, and I loved it. During this time I became involved with many political, peace and social justice causes, and even got arrested at a military weapons exhibition protest one day in 1979. After getting arrested I spent the night in the Orange County Jail. From that time on, I felt free. It really was "The System" that was insane, not me. My political freedom and activism from then on became my savior, my therapy.

Several of my jail mates in the Orange County jail that night were Unitarian Church peace activists who had come down from their church in Los Angeles to get arrested with us in Orange County. From them I learned of the existence of another Unitarian Church in Anaheim, a radical liberal church, located just a few blocks from where I lived. I'd never heard of them. They were an amazing congregation. Many of them were older east coast, leftist political radicals, who had migrated to Orange County during the fifties and sixties, taking the jobs that were then so plentiful, especially for engineers, teachers and other professionals. They settled into Orange County's suburbia; an area that was very white and extremely right wing; often a bigoted, anti-Semitic, and racist kind of place. Seeking solace and companionship, they came together to form this anachronistic radical leftist church in defiance of the ultra-right-wing politics they had moved into. It wasn't long after the church's foundation in the mid-fifties, when the local John Birch Society and their ilk began referring to the Unitarian Church of Orange County as "that Communist Church." I became a dedicated member and very involved with them and their activities for the next twenty years.

|||

In the spring of 1983, I sold a print shop I had established a few years earlier and decided to take a break to hit the road for a while and take a long-range vagabond-style bicycle trip to Canada. I drug out and dusted off my old ten-speed bike. After several trips to the local REI Co-op store, I outfitted my bike for the trip with everything necessary to hit the road. Fifteen years before in nineteen sixty-eight I had taken off on a hitch-hiking trip north to try to get to Canada to try to escape the Vietnam War. Something was driving me to want to go back in time; something existed within me that needed to be recovered.

I hit the road north again. This time it would be a solo bicycle journey of nearly fifteen hundred miles that would take more than eight weeks to complete. On Memorial Day 1983, I took off alone with my bike and equipment which weighed more than a hundred pounds. I rode the coast north for a few days until I got to Santa Barbara where I found a phone booth and called an old family friend who still lived there. Henry immediately invited me over and offered his backyard where I set up my backpacker's tent. I stayed for a few very enjoyable days and nights, bike-touring and rediscovering the historic and beautiful old city of Santa Barbara where I was born in 1948; exploring the city by bicycle during the days and socializing with Henry and his family in the evenings.

From there I rode north along the Pacific Coast Highway, usually averaging thirty-five or forty miles a day, camping at county or state parks along the way. I was self-contained and self-sufficient, with all I needed packed carefully within my bicycle's panniers. During this trip I stayed with friends and relatives and enjoyed their welcoming hospitality. Those eight weeks on the road became a time of total release and self-discovery as I physically and mentally pumped my bicycle over many miles of territory, through high mountain ranges and so much of the beauty that the northwest pacific region beholds.

Along the way I kept thinking of my experience of going north some fifteen years earlier when I was then trying to escape the Vietnam War (see Chapter 8 – Going North) by escaping to Canada. I was somehow trying to recover or get back to something I'd left behind; something I wasn't done with. Spending the days and nights on the road for those weeks, with nothing going on but my heart, lungs, and my legs pumping, had really calmed my mind into a space of peaceful serenity and awareness. The time on the road with myself left me with a lot of time to contemplate things and I began to fantasize about other possible future ventures; I conjured up an idea of returning someday to Vietnam on some kind of peace mission.

That summer was a very wet summer in the pacific north-west and I was getting repeatedly soaked and hammered by rainstorms, so by the time I rode into Seattle, I decided to call it quits. I rode up to a bike shop just south of Seattle and traded in my old worn out bike for twenty bucks and a ride to the airport where I caught the red-eye flight back home to LA.

CHAPTER FIFTY-SIX

Political Activism

I HADN'T READ or listened to the news while out on my eight-week bicycling journey. It was a few days before I flew home from Seattle when I came into a diner for breakfast and bought a newspaper from a news stand.

"US Naval Forces Prepare to Invade Nicaragua and Central America."

I wondered if this was the lead-up to another Vietnam-style war. This was August of 1983, early in the Ronald Reagan administration, when secret American agents worked to assist and enable the organization of military "Death Squads" in El Salvador and other nations in Central America; this to control popular uprisings of peasants, workers unions, and students who were organizing against the dictators in power who were continuously oppressing them. The story was a familiar one.

Within a few weeks after flying home from my bike trip, I gathered a few friends of mine at the Unitarian Church and convened the first meeting of a political organization that became known as "The Orange County Committee on Central America" (OCCOCA). Our goals were to study what was happening in Central America and do all that we could to expose it, then to oppose and resist what we saw as another Vietnam War gaining traction. We organized our committee in order to educate our community about what our country seemed to be planning again; another imperialist military invasion, an assault being orchestrated by many of the same game players who had brought us the atrocity of Vietnam.

The Committee chose me to be its chairman, and I was one of three who led the group. Doctor Shirley Ceranti, served as vice-chair. She was a recently retired Professor Emerita of Sociology from one of our local universities, was a widely respected Marxist intellectual who had developed quite a following within leftist lecture circles around the country. The other chair was Al Abrams, old enough to be my father, was a life-long Socialist through and through, with an incredible political history of his own. With the three of us leading, OCCOCA quickly grew from a small group of just a few, to hundreds of activists in Orange County where we held weekly meetings at the Unitarian Church to strategize and plan our group's activities. We became successful as a local grassroots "Central American Solidarity" organization. Our members became involved with and led congressional delegations to Central America. We activated or worked in concert with students organizing on several colleges in Orange County, often organizing public events on campuses where we would showcase speakers, films, and cultural educational activities. We also became involved with the religious community where we did much of the same.

At the time, many Central Americans, mostly from El Salvador, were living without documents in the poorer neighborhoods of Orange County, where they had come running for their lives for sanctuary to escape brutal persecutions in their home countries; conditions that were created by American foreign policy. Many of them had been student or labor union activists who had simply sought to improve the impoverishment of their families' situations, only to become listed on Death Squad lists for extermination. American foreign policymakers during that time were collaborating with the tyrannical governments of those countries who labeled and targeted these innocents as "communists" to be killed. It all had the look and smell of Vietnam all over again.

Our group made special efforts to seek out and introduce our committee to those Central Americans who had fled their persecutions and sought sanctuary in Orange County. We welcomed these people into our committee meetings, which were held bilingually in English and Spanish. They were grateful to us for allowing their stories to be told. They spoke to us in emotional detail of their horrifying personal experiences with the death squads and their efforts to escape and survive. They shared their lives and we encouraged them to become leading members of our organization which they did.

Throughout the remainder of the eighties, the wars wore on in El Salvador, Guatemala, Honduras, Nicaragua, and the rest of Central America while our country became lost in the "Reagan Revolution." President Ronald Reagan and his right-wing agenda brutally pursued these wars which murdered untold thousands of innocent civilians in the region. He became greatly admired by many right-wing Republican Americans during his terms, yet widely criticized and condemned internationally for his criminal activities and involvement in things like the Iran-Contra Affair, and other military madness. I believe the collective efforts of the Central American activists worldwide - that we were involved with - did stop the region from becoming another Vietnam.

In time, I went back to work as an employee again; working to pay my mortgage; working to take care of my kids; letting things go by for several years.

CHAPTER FIFTY-SEVEN

Operation Desert Storm

IN 1991, THE Gulf War and "Operation Desert Storm" came along. It was nothing other than the latest attempt by US oil corporations to use our military to violently move in and take control of the vast oil reserves in that region for their own profits. The excuse for this war was that the dictator of Iraq, Saddam Hussein, had sent his Army across its border into the neighboring nation of Kuwait to take control of their massive underground oil reserves. What was hardly mentioned in the press was that the United States had worked to empower Saddam Hussein in the first place as a means to get back at the Muslim Ayatollahs in Iran who had taken over that country and expelled American oil corporations.

I saw this Gulf War as another unnecessary conflict our country was willing to become involved in, with no other apparent purpose than to fill the pockets of the rich and greedy. The American War in Vietnam came about because of the power and influence of those who controlled our economic system. The same old story was being played out again. Ownership of the world's resources and labor has always been at play, and the wealth to be gained from control of these has always been the struggle. The capitalist ownership class has always been determined to dominate and control the world's wealth whenever and however it can, ultimately through violent military means.

I recognized that as a veteran I had a special platform from which to speak against the war. I attended an Orange County anti-war demonstration, where I was interviewed by a local reporter from the *Orange County Register* and quoted in the paper with my anti-war views. The reporter emphasized that I was a Vietnam Veteran speaking up and against this war. What she especially liked about me was that I was wearing on my lapel a large anti-war button featuring Bart Simpson with the quote, "Make Love, Not War." This article drew public attention and soon I was contacted by an old friend who wanted to organize something to be called "Orange County Veterans for Peace,"; a way to organize other Orange County veterans who wanted to speak out and respond to this latest act of US military aggression.

A national veterans organization, much smaller than the American Legion or the Veterans of Foreign Wars (VFW), Veterans for Peace is composed of military veterans who stand apart from these other organizations. They actually stand for peace and in opposition to war. We formed our chapter and organized protests in Orange County, in concert with local and Los Angeles County peace organizations and other national anti-war coalitions. Our goal was to awaken public consciousness and opinion to resist the war. Our slogan was "No Blood for Oil!" The national and worldwide anti-war movement was huge; we organized, protested, and marched by the millions to oppose the war to little effect.

In the end, hundreds of thousands of young, innocent Iraqi

soldiers were mercilessly mowed down in the desert by US sky pilots; military madness had its way once again as it had done in Vietnam. The killing was intense, and it went on and on. Most Americans never blinked an eye. Our local VFP chapter grew, and I became more and more involved with Veterans for Peace over the next few years.

CHAPTER FIFTY-EIGHT

Tony

DURING MY ANTI-WAR activity, I became friends with a very special person named Anthony "Tony" Russo. I met Tony while acting as the program director of the Orange County Unitarian Church. I'd heard he was a good anti-war speaker, speaking out against this useless war so I invited him to speak to our congregation one Sunday morning. He had an incredible past and was a gentle, peaceful kind of soul. I liked him immediately.

It was two decades before I met Tony, in 1971, that he became famous, or infamous to some, for his efforts to release to the American public something that came to be known as "The Pentagon Papers." These papers were held in secret and the public was not allowed to even know of their existence.

In June 1967, Robert S. McNamara, the defense secretary, set up the Vietnam Study Task Force, ultimately employing a large working group of analysts and historians, to prepare a classified history of the Vietnam War from 1945 to 1967. In dozens of volumes it revealed conversations at the highest levels of government that sometimes directly contradicted official statements, including the timing and the scale of the United States' troop buildup. Tony Russo was one of these analysts, hired by the CIA-connected RAND Corporation, which was under contract to produce the history. He was sent to Vietnam during the war to interview Viet Cong prisoners and it was during this time that he met Daniel Ellsberg who was also involved with the study.

Having access to the papers and knowing full well that the American public was being lied to about the Vietnam war, they made a pact with each other to reveal the truth. They then copied the papers and released them to the *New York Times* and the *Washington Post*. The shit hit the fan as the country woke to the truth. They were jailed and initially charged with conspiracy, espionage, and theft of government property. The charges were later dismissed after prosecutors investigating the Watergate Scandal discovered that staff members in the Nixon White House had ordered the so-called White House Plumbers to engage in unlawful efforts to discredit Tony and Ellsberg. The judge threw the case out.

This ordeal took place in the early seventies, but it was not until about twenty years later that Tony and I met and became friends. We would get together over lunch and talk for hours about our personal experiences in Vietnam; mine as an Army medic and ambulance driver on the ground in Vietnam during those times and his as a Rand Corporation / CIA interrogator of Viet Cong prisoners of war. We shared the stories of our mutually understood experiences. He told me he'd interrogated many young Vietnamese men who'd left their homelands in the north to travel south by foot through hundreds of miles of extremely dangerous jungle pathways, often barefoot, loaded with heavy weaponry to deliver to their comrades in the south of Vietnam, in hopes of killing the American invaders. I told him the story of the time I had loaded up an ambulance full of wounded Viet Cong soldiers to be delivered to the prison in Saigon to await their fate. There were hundreds and thousands of these young Vietnamese soldiers who wanted to do this even though they knew they had little chance of survival. This is what they lived and died for. As an interrogator, it was easy for Tony to see there was no way for America to win when the average American soldier ordered to Vietnam couldn't give a shit about the war. The average soldier definitely didn't want to die there. Most American men resented being sent there and wanted to come home. The outcome of the war was obvious, and the truth was being held from the American public.

When he completed his assignment in Vietnam for the Department of Defense and the RAND Corporation, Tony returned home and dedicated his life to informing the American public about the truth in Vietnam. Because of his heroic efforts to expose to the American public the lies we had all been fed to keep the war going, Tony suffered greatly. After it became known that he was behind the release of the Pentagon Papers, he was arrested, taken into prison and treated horribly. With tears in his eyes he emotionally told me of the details. They beat him and stomped upon his feet and toes. Even after the charges were dropped against him and Ellsberg, and they were released from jail, Nixon's goons continued to stalk and threaten him on the streets of Santa Monica. He remains one of the great unsung American heroes – a man who has never been recognized as such. He brought the truth to us. Tony strongly believed that those of us who knew what others didn't had the duty – the obligation - to speak truth to power.

CHAPTER FIFTY-NINE

Returning to Vietnam

IT WAS THE summer of 1993, twenty-three years after I left the American War in Vietnam that I found myself in Saigon, speaking in an auditorium to a large crowd. I poured my heart and soul out in explaining why I was there. I told them, through an interpreter, that I had once been drafted and forced, against my will, to go to Vietnam and participate in the war that they referred to as "The American War." I told them I would always try to explain to Americans that America had illegally invaded Vietnam. It was a war that eventually resulted in the unnecessary genocidal killing of over three million Vietnamese. They listened to me carefully and understood and appreciated every word I said.

|||

Earlier that spring, while serving as President of the Orange County Chapter of Veterans for Peace, I responded to an invitation from a guy associated with a northern California VFP Chapter; an effort they were organizing to send Vietnam

War Veterans back to Vietnam. A Vietnam Veteran, Fredy Champagne, had been organizing trips back to Vietnam for Vietnam Veterans in an effort to help then reconcile the war, and find peace within themselves. It was announced as an opportunity for Vietnam Veterans to engage in a "Peace Walk in Vietnam," a chance for peace and self-healing, a chance for reconciliation with our former enemies. I liked the idea and realized I needed to do that, so I contacted Fredy, and accepted the offer and invitation.

This Peace Walk was to be a citizens' diplomatic mission with two simple specific goals in mind:

WE SHALL CALL FOR THE END TO THE US ECONOMIC EMBARGO OF VIETNAM!

WE SHALL CALL FOR THE NORMALIZATION OF RELATIONS BETWEEN OUR TWO COUNTRIES!

After America was defeated in Vietnam in 1975, our government continued to wage a vengeful economic war against the Vietnamese people and their government. During this time, America did its best to make sure Vietnam could not take part in international trade organizations like the International Monetary Fund (IMF) or the World Trade Organization (WTO). Our governmental policy was such that it strangled Vietnam economically and continued to make them suffer. This policy of vengeance caused many people in Vietnam to live in squalid conditions of poverty. There were some of us veterans who knew what was still going on in Vietnam and were determined to do something about it.

On June 19 1993 I gathered with several Vietnam Veterans and other peace activists at the Los Angeles International Airport. This journey was to become a profound high point of my life; an opportunity to set things right after so many years.

Before the trip, I worked for weeks with Fredy Champagne

and other activists, collecting and preparing a ton and a half of donated medical supplies for us to check as personal luggage to present to the people of Vietnam as gifts when we arrived. Every traveler in our group carried two seventy-pound boxes of medical supplies.

In 1993, the American government did not allow its citizens to travel freely to Vietnam. You couldn't just get on an airplane and fly there. It was illegal under US State Department law to travel there with more than two hundred US dollars. Of course, our medical supplies were worth thousands and to take them into Vietnam was considered by our State Department to be a crime. To circumvent these restrictions, we flew out of Los Angeles on Malaysian Air to Kuala Lumpur, Malaysia. After spending the night there, we transferred ourselves and our medical supplies and flew directly into Hanoi, the capital city of Vietnam. Coming into Hanoi was a surreal sight. Circling above the city before landing, I could plainly see the lunar-like crater landscape below that had been created by American bombing missions during the war, still present after twenty-three years. It was devastating.

The Peace Walk in Vietnam began in central Hanoi the next day on Tuesday, July 20, 1993, at 5pm at the headquarters of the Union of Peace, Friendship and Solidarity Organizations. Prior to the start of the walk, a banner was unfurled which read—

"Forward! Together in Friendship! Vietnam/USA Peace Walk 93."

We marched behind this banner. Former Vietnamese and American soldiers, we marched down Quan Than St. where we ended our march at Lake Concourse, in the heart of Hanoi. They carried American flags, and we carried Vietnamese flags. We were all there together, former enemies, marching for peace and reconciliation.

The war was over!

After taking control in 1975, the Communist government of Vietnam rarely allowed public demonstrations of any kind, but our delegation was allowed to do so. Many local, foreign, and independent press correspondents including the Vietnam News Agency, Vietnam Television, *Saigon Times*, Reuters, Kyoto News Agency, the Afro-Asian Press and AP were present to witness and report this. They interviewed me several times that day, and I spoke the plain truth about why I was there. I told them it was time to put the Vietnam War behind us and create lasting peace. It was time to reconcile the people of the United States of America with the people of Vietnam. Later that day, our delegation, amongst speeches, presented our gifts of the ton and a half of medical supplies we'd brought along, to our hosts, the Vietnam Peace Committee. They were all so grateful and, in return, they showered us with national Vietnamese praise and attention. We became media stars in Vietnam and in other parts of the world for the next three weeks! The American press mostly ignored us, of course. Our delegation remained in Hanoi for several days, where we were hosted by government officials at several political media events.

One day, our guides took us out into the surrounding countryside so we could experience a bit of the cultural history and richness of Vietnamese life. They took us to an ancient mountain farming village that still maintained their way of life as they had done for hundreds, if not thousands, of years. Along the way, as we drove through country hamlets in our air-conditioned vans, I asked our guides what damage American bombers had done to each hamlet and how many innocent elderly people, women, and children had been killed by our bombing during the war. In each neighborhood, they provided exact answers. Twenty were exterminated here, forty-three were burnt alive there. It went on and on. During America's war against the people of Vietnam, more than three million Vietnamese people died. The majority were innocent civilians killed because of the war that the United States waged against them.

After we left the tribal village, I asked our Vietnamese guides if there was a veteran's home in the area where we could visit to pay our respects. They conferred amongst themselves for a while, then reported that there was such an opportunity, but it would take a few hours to arrange. We got off the road and waited in the shade in the countryside.

We arrived in our vans later that afternoon to a desolate-looking place in the Vietnamese mountain countryside just south of Vietnam's border with China. It was a ramshackle collection of pitiful, broken-down buildings, far away from the rest of Vietnam, way out in the countryside. We pulled up to the veteran's center where its commanding officer, Colonel Vu, wearing a western-style white shirt and tie, warmly greeted us and invited us in. I could plainly see that this dilapidated veteran's home was a place of misery for the hundreds of Vietnamese war veterans who had to live there in a terrible state of poverty. I don't know how many of these poor men were sent to live out the remaining years of their lives there. It most likely was many thousands. Many were missing limbs and eyes or suffering brain injuries because of America's relentless and criminal assault on their country. These poor veterans had nothing. The poverty of their condition was apparent. This was the very cruel reality for which our delegation was there to somehow make amends.

The Colonel invited us into a meeting room where we

all sat down around a large prearranged wooden table to talk about our purpose there. Seated around the table were about a dozen Americans, accompanied by our officially appointed Vietnamese government guides and interpreters. On the other side of the table sat the Colonel and an equal number of disabled Vietnamese war veterans who lived at the center. Our hosts provided beer and snacks of cashews for us to enjoy before we began our conversations. It was a special occasion for them, and they were curious. They wanted to know why we were there.

Preparing for my trip back to Vietnam, I'd printed, in Vietnamese, a thousand business cards with our Veterans for Peace logo on the front side. On the back side of the card, I had typeset in Vietnamese very simply why I was there,

"I am here as a former American War Veteran to put the American war behind us and to find Peace and Reconciliation between our two nations - To end the economic war and to establish diplomatic relations."

We were Veterans for Peace.

I passed the cards out and they took a few minutes to carefully read them. Soon I saw smiles of understanding come over their faces and it was then our discussions began. As they realized where we were coming from, we became brothers right there in that room together. We drank and wept as our Vietnamese guides and interpreters looked on and enabled us to communicate with each other. This was one of the most significant experiences of my life. I was drenched in emotion. We then took part in roundtable discussions where each of us freely expressed ourselves. When it came my turn to speak, I explained to them I was a very young man when I was drafted and ordered to go to Vietnam though I was against the war. My situation was that I had to accept conscription or go to prison.

I then volunteered to serve as a medical corpsman in hopes that I could save rather than kill.

It was then that Colonel Vu, through our interpreter, asked me,

"When and where did you serve while in the war?"

I told him that for most of my time in the war I operated out of a base camp that we Americans called "Bearcat," near the village of Long Thanh in "South Vietnam." I was there for much of 1969, working as an Army medic and ambulance driver. I saw his eyes light up. Our eyes met.

I then asked the Colonel when and where he served during the war. He told me he had served during the war at the very same time and place I had served. He was on the other side of the war, a commanding officer in charge of the Communist military forces that were our enemy at the time with their dedicated goal of repulsing and killing the Americans who had invaded their country.

The memories came back to me in a flood of those long months in Bearcat in 1969 when, night after night, our artillery and airpower had poured unbelievable death and destruction upon those who were determined to defend their homeland. Our forces massacred them. I witnessed it. Night after night, they tried to attack us, but they really had nothing to work with. I witnessed their demise just outside our perimeter on a nightly basis. Our air power and artillery slaughtered them, and I'd wept for them as they had little chance of survival.

The decades had gone on and it was now just me and the Colonel facing each other. We wept. I expressed to him and our group my memories of that time and the sorrowful effect it had on me. It was then that he and I got up, removed ourselves from our chairs, and came together in an embrace, removing the pain of the past. Tears were flowing. We had forgiven and established peace.

I passed these cards out. On the back of them, written in Vietnamese, was this message –

"I am here as an American War veteran to put the American War behind us and find Peace and Reconciliation between our two nations – I am here to end the economic war and to establish diplomatic relations."

Mama San

*On our Peace Walk in 1993 we visited a place
known as Marble Mountain near China Beach
which is just south of Da Nang. This elderly Vietnamese
woman who, as a young woman, had been raped by American
soldiers during war still feared Americans, but she allowed
me to take her photo from which I painted this portrait.*

Water Buffalo

*One day we pulled off the road in the countryside
and visited a cemetery located within the forest under a
triple deck canopy of trees. Very quiet and sad, there were
thousands of graves, mostly of those who had been
killed in the war. I was standing there, paying my respects,
when out of the corner of my eye I noticed a large form
beginning to move in front of me. This Vietnamese
water buffalo farm animal stared at me.*

Orphans

While in Nha Trang, I asked our guides if they could take me to an orphanage where I could make a donation. The front rows of children pictured here are from photos taken at that orphanage. This painting is a montage of images representing what America's wars and all wars always do. It depicts what it did to so many Vietnamese children.

Coconut Stand

*Taking a coconut milk break on the side of the
road just north of Ho Chi Minh City*

Begging Children, Nga Trang, 1993

Hungry and impoverished children often begged us for anything we could give them.

CHAPTER SIXTY

The Vietnam Dream

WHEN OUR PEACE Walk delegation arrived in Vietnam in July of 1993, it was evident the people on the street in Hanoi and all over the country were impoverished and starving. Within a few months after we returned from Vietnam, diplomatic relations between our nations were beginning to be restored. Our group was just one small part – only a platoon-sized effort, within a large-scale effort to help bring some prosperity to that country. Within a few years, Vietnam became one of the United States' favorite trading partners. Ten years after that, the average Vietnamese person weighed twenty pounds more. I am proud of that fact.

|||

Once upon a time, many decades ago, the most powerful nation on Earth, The United States of America, decided to intervene in the affairs of the tiny nation Vietnam, a very small and poor, yet sovereign nation, to impose its will there. This intervention was organized and conducted from the top down by America's political, military, and business classes, with little input or say from those at the bottom who would be the ones to go there; to fight and die. This misguided intervention eventually collapsed and came crashing down. Our Peace Walk was a simple grassroots effort generated from the ground up; an intervention empowered by the most powerful energy known to man; the desire to love and care for our fellow man. Our intervention was a success while our governments was a monumental, disastrous, failure.

This story began early in my life where I described many experiences that influenced me and formed my character, but it mostly takes off from the summer of 1963, when I first became aware of a country called Vietnam. My story ends thirty years later when I flew out of Vietnam in the summer of 1993. The experience of going back left me mentally and physically exhausted and it took a few months to recover, but it was the best thing I have ever done.

| | |

As I flew out of Saigon, I wrote this poem

"A SONG ARISES"

As we walk for Peace
In Vietnam
A Song Arises
It rises from the Red Earth
In Long Thanh

And it winds around my soul
Like a flowered covered vine

It comes from the People

From village to village
From city to city
From the mountain people
In the north
To the people of Cu Chi
In the south

And the song is constant
Like a driving Monsoon rain
Singing in the language
That has no words
But washes our spirits
And renews our hopes
And Understanding

For Peace is on the Way
And flying in the hearts
Of both of our nations

For Peace is on the Way
Into the heart of the world
That Awaits us

It cannot be stopped

JIM GIBSON

POSTSCRIPT

I HAVE COME a long way since my return visit to Vietnam in 1993. After returning from the trip I sought therapy and help for my condition of PTSD and received it. Facing my demons proved to be the right thing to do as the ensuing years of my life have proven to be much happier and productive.

|||

Today, the Communists who defeated us in 1975 remain in charge in Vietnam and control the economy while supplying American consumers with vast amounts of many kinds of products they manufacture; Clothing and Textiles, Footwear and Electronics. They have become one of the United States' favorite trading partners and their workers have displaced American workers by the millions. It is much more profitable for American billionaire capitalists to source their labor from Vietnam and other Asian countries; conspiring to take the profits, still leaving most Vietnamese workers to remain in poverty as in the past. Our working class has taken a huge dive since our nation became involved in the Vietnam War. You would think the ownership class would have done this in the first place without having to waste more than fifty-eight-thousand American soldiers' lives in an unnecessary war; wiping out so much of our country financially and emotionally; killing more than three million Vietnamese in the process.

The Vietnam War, is regarded by many as the worst mistake, or worst crime, America has ever committed. But what have we learned? Our country is just now, extricating itself from another, long, costly, unnecessary 'Vietnam War-like' intervention, in Afghanistan. Our System keeps involving us in these wars, so it seems we haven't learned much. Even worse, there is a threat arising that America has never faced before; a Constitutional crisis beyond compare.

In the past, the System just overthrew the governments of other sovereign states when it felt it was in its interest to do so. That was something done to other nations, but we didn't allow it here.

That very "System," behind the various coups in Vietnam and all the other coups it has staged around the world, has just attempted to do the same to us here at home. America has just barely survived an internal military coup attempt orchestrated by a would-be dictator and his right-wing fascist supporters who make up nearly half of our voting population. It is uncertain how long our republic can hold on. Democracy may be a fleeting thing for America as we seem more confused than ever.

World events are changing at a radically, dizzying, fast pace. Our global climate is rapidly melting down putting the very existence of humanity in doubt. A horrible pandemic has killed us by the hundreds of thousands. Americans have perished needlessly because so many have given in to fear and cynicism; tossing science and reason to the side and choosing instead to support authoritarian tyranny and conspiracy theories. So many cannot seem to wake from their confusion while our democratic system comes under attack by a fascist mentality.

Everything once again feels as if it is coming apart, causing me to look back to a time when I had similar feelings. The social turmoil of the sixties, occurred not so long ago. The callous racism, bigoted ignorance, and disregard for human life that I first became so aware of during my younger years still flourishes. Where will it lead? We don't know exactly what is going to happen. The future is uncertain, but it is in our hands. We are on a journey into the unknown and I think this is the basic truth of our existence – we just try to make the best of things as they come to us. We must use our minds, and we must do our best. All of us in our own way are trying to make it back home alive just as so many young American soldiers struggled to do, so long ago in Vietnam. Time will tell if America can save itself.

I believe we shall survive and live on.

Jim Gibson
September 15, 2021
Laguna Woods, Ca.

Made in the USA
Columbia, SC
14 March 2022

57511207R10183